# THE CATHOLIC PRAYER BOOK

# The Catholic Prayer Book

Compiled by Msgr. Michael Buckley
Edited by Tony Castle

First published in 1984 in Great Britain by Hodder and Stoughton
First American Edition 1986 by Servant
An Imprint of Viident

*Concordat cum originali:* John P. Dewis
*Imprimatur:* Rt. Rev. Thomas McMahon, Bishop of Brentwood,
30 April, 1984

Book and cover design by Mark Sullivan
Cover image © iStockphoto | chatchaisurakram



Library of Congress Cataloging-in-Publication Data
The Catholic prayer book / compiled by Msgr. Michael Buckley ; edited by Tony Castle.
pages cm
Includes bibliographical references and index.
ISBN 978-1-61636-610-0 (pbk. : alk. paper) — ISBN 978-1-61636-611-7 (leatherette : alk. paper)
1. Catholic Church—Prayers and devotions. I. Buckley, Michael, 1924- editor of compilation. II. Castle, Tony, 1938- editor of compilation. III. Title.
BX2130.T74 2013
242›.802—dc23
2012051044

ISBN: 978-1-63582-348-6 (softcover)
ISBN: 978-1-61636-611-7 (leatherette edition)
ISBN: 978-1-63582-302-8 (eBook)

The acknowledgments starting on page 317 constitute an extension of this copyright page.

Printed in the United States of America

10 9 8 7 6 5 4 3 2 1

# CONTENTS

**Foreword** | *7*

**Introduction** | *9*

**How to Use this Prayer Book** | *13*

**Prayer: The Christian Vocation** | *17*

**Prayers to God the Father** | *19*
*Prayers of Thanksgiving* | *19*
*Prayers of Praise* | *22*

**Prayers to God the Son** | *36*

**Prayers to the Holy Spirit** | *65*
*For the Presence of the Holy Spirit* | *65*
*For the Gifts of the Holy Spirit* | *70*

**Praying the Sacraments** | *72*

**Baptism and Confirmation** | *74*
*Prayers for Baptism* | *74*
*Prayers for Confirmation* | *78*

**The Eucharist: Sacrifice and Sacrament** | *79*

**The Sacrifice of the Mass** | *81*
*Prayers Before Mass* | *81*
*The Order of Mass* | *87*
*Prayers After Mass* | *127*

**The Blessed Sacrament** | *129*
*Prayers Before Holy Communion* | *129*
*Prayers After Holy Communion* | *135*
*Prayers Before the Blessed Sacrament* | *139*
*Eucharistic Exposition* | *151*
*Eucharistic Benediction* | *152*

**Reconciliation** | *159*
*Prayers Before Receiving the Sacrament of Reconciliation* | *161*
*Prayers After Receiving the Sacrament of Reconciliation* | *166*

**A Life of Prayer** | *169*

**Daily Prayers** | *172*
*General Prayers* | *172*
*Short Acts* | *175*
*At the Day's Beginning* | *176*
*At the Day's Close* | *194*

**Family Prayer** | *206*

**Praying Continually** | *214*

**Prayers for Special Needs** | *224*
*For the Church* | *224*
*For the Body of Christ* | *225*
*For the World* | *228*
*For Workers* | *233*
*For the Suffering, Sick, and Dying* | *235*
*For Travelers* | *237*
*For Spiritual Growth* | *239*
*For the Inner Life* | *247*
*In Times of Trial* | *251*
*For Others* | *252*
*In Times of Sickness and Healing* | *257*

**Prayers to Mary, Mother of the Church** | *270*
*Prayers to Our Lady* | *270*
*The Rosary* | *280*

**Prayers to the Angels and Saints** | *292*

**Prayers for the Holy Souls** | *307*

**Acknowledgments** | *317*

# FOREWORD

My esteemed predecessor, John Cardinal O'Connor, described *The Catholic Prayer Book* as "compiled with a sense of that unique devotion which has characterized Catholic piety through the ages and yet it is thoroughly contemporary." The solid core of well tested Catholic prayers is complemented by prayers and reflections by modern spiritual writers and others.

Msgr. Buckley's collection is notable for its generous use of the *Roman Missal*. Central texts, such as the Gloria, Creed, and Eucharistic prayers are provided, along with those related to Exposition of the Blessed Sacrament and Benediction. Prayers by St. Ambrose and St. Thomas Aquinas, which the *Roman Missal* offers for the priest's preparation for and thanksgiving following Mass, are here made easily accessible to all. Within the chapter containing prayers for special occasions, over forty powerful and succinct orations from the *Missal* are followed by more than one hundred and fifty additional texts drawn from a wide variety of sources.

*The Catholic Prayer Book* manifests a loving attentiveness to the person of Our Lord, devotion to the Father, and to the Holy Spirit. It offers paths to a deeper encounter with the unity of the Church through prayers addressed to Our Lady, to St. Joseph, the angels, and others among the blessed.

Along with my esteemed predecessor, I highly endorse *The Catholic Prayer Book*.

Cardinal Timothy Dolan
Archbishop of New York

# INTRODUCTION

Prayer is as natural to us as breathing. For Christians both are necessary for life. The way in which we Christians pray reflects our spirituality and belief. Jesus is the center of our prayer life, as he directs our thoughts and actions to God our Father. We pray in the power of the Holy Spirit.

The special emphasis we give in our prayers reflects the particular Christian church to which we belong. The Eastern Church, for example, highlights the "otherness" of God by its emphasis on the Holy Spirit as the great sanctifying force in our lives. The Church of England has a very strong establishment influence in its set prayers, while non-conformist churches tend toward a more spontaneous form of open prayer. Roman Catholic spirituality, on the other hand, while not excluding any of these elements in its prayer life, lays great emphasis on the devotional aspect of our prayerful relationship with God.

Catholic prayer books, with their well-thumbed pages, were the treasured possession of Catholics for centuries. A prayer book given as a present to mark a special occasion, such as First Communion, confirmation, or marriage, remained with the Catholic all through life. It represented part of his or her heritage. These prayer books were interlaced with special prayer cards, of personal spiritual significance to the owner, which told the story of his life and pilgrimage as a Christian. In one sense they were as revered by the Catholic as the Bible by a Protestant.

As Catholics today we are in danger of losing much of what is best and beautiful in our spirituality. This is due indeliberately in large part to the Second Vatican Council, with its emphasis on the need for renewal and relevance in Catholic teaching and practice. This bad side effect of ignoring, or even rejecting, traditional Catholic prayers was not the council's intention, but it is in fact what happened.

In a desire to update Catholic spirituality, and bring it into line with the new ecumenical thinking, there was a tendency for contemporary Catholic prayer books to pay scant, if any, attention to the prayers of a former age. These new prayer books not only were not Catholic prayer books as we knew them but were scarcely distinguishable from other prayer books, even those not specifically Christian. Their main criterion was that authentic prayer must come from present-day life. In the process many of our beautiful old prayers, hallowed by use, were discarded. The fact that they had sustained countless millions in their spiritual lives was ignored, and thus many hallowed Catholic practices fell by the wayside. It is in an attempt to restore the balance that *The Catholic Prayer Book* has been compiled.

Because spirituality is an ongoing process, this prayer book contains, we hope, a selection of the best contemporary prayers that will probably stand the test of time. Many old prayers that are of great intrinsic spiritual value have been updated in order to clarify their true meaning for us today. (An asterisk next to a source's name indicates that the prayer has been adapted.)

In the heat of the Reformation too, there was a tendency to overstress some aspects of Catholic doctrine and spirituality so that we could be clearly distinguished from our separated brethren. This difference has not been diluted but has been placed in its true setting, either by the use of contemporary language or by a less strident proclamation of our belief. The adaptation of the prayers has been lit up by the Church's teaching on the Resurrection and the power of the Holy Spirit constantly at work in the Church through all the ages, including our own.

Many beautiful old prayers, however, defy adaptation and remain in their original form because they are so clearly the work of the Spirit. They trip off the tongue because we know them not only by heart but in our hearts as well.

Some prayers have been specially composed to fit the mood of our spirituality in those sections that needed amplification. This gives a more complete and rounded effect, so that each section dovetails into the rest.

The Church is spiritually one. In this it reflects the unity of the Trinity. But we live, in fact, in a fragmented Church and world. We believe that the Spirit pours out his gifts on all those in the Church who confess Jesus as Lord to the glory of the Father. *The Catholic Prayer Book*, therefore, in acknowledging this diversity of spiritual gifts of the Spirit to all the members of Christ's Church, incorporates in its pages many prayers of Christian denominations other than Catholic. We appreciate the Spirit at work in the lives of Christians through prayer. In this way the prayer book reflects our ecumenical age and deepens our Catholic spirituality. When we pray together as Christians, we are taking the best possible steps on the road to unity.

Our awareness of the diversity of the gifts of the Spirit makes us acknowledge also that we still have a lot to learn from other Christian heritages. We therefore approach the Father in prayer in a spirit of humility and wonder. Accordingly we hope that other Christian churches will use this prayer book, not only to gain a fuller awareness of our Catholic prayer life but also to deepen their own. We have a common Father, one mediator, and the same Spirit at work in all of us. *The Catholic Prayer Book* is for all Christians and not just for Catholics.

## HOW TO USE THIS PRAYER BOOK

*Prayer is basically personal. It is as unique to each one of us as our fingerprints. It is a one-to-one relationship with God my loving Father, and it is all about my life with him. So in a sense, it is impossible to write a book of prayers for someone else. But however personal it may be, true Christian prayer has certain basic common strands because it involves the community from which no one is excluded.*

In the final analysis only the Spirit of God can teach us how to pray or give us the words in which to express our needs and deepest spiritual feelings (see Romans 8:26–27). He prays in and through us. Without him we cannot pray. How each individual uses this prayer book depends on his or her unique situation and present relationship with God and the community. No hard or fast set of rules can be laid down, because we are dealing with matters of the Spirit.

In prayer we live the life of the Blessed Trinity. It is for this reason that the prayer book begins with a section on prayers to the Father, Son, and Holy Spirit. This sets the tone of our spirituality and our Christian vocation.

Catholic devotion is centered on the sacraments, which are our personal encounter with Christ. The keystone of our worship is the Eucharist, in which Christ is both our victim and our spiritual food. The prayers in this book help us to live out more fully our sacramental life and worship.

The final section contains prayers for every aspect of our Christian lives, so that at all times and in all circumstances we live in the presence of God the Father, Son, and Holy Spirit.

The prayer book will afford us starting points for individual or group prayer. Just as a plane, to be airborne, needs a launching pad, so also this prayer book may help to lead us into prayerful conversation with God. It is a means to an end. The end is to be with God, especially in praise and thanksgiving.

Just as there are times spent in talking, so there are also times for listening to God in prayer. What he says to us is much more important than what we say to him. Prayer is not a matter of talking a great deal but of loving a great deal. It is thinking about God while loving him and loving him while thinking about him. Silence, for the Christian, is not just the absence of speech but the stillness of soul in which our true self is united with its Creator and Father. We become silent in awe and wonder, as we contemplate God within us. It is an experience too rich and sensitive for words.

But because we are human, we use words, and this is where *The Catholic Prayer Book* meets a need. Here we find formal prayers for any time of day and any event of our lives, because everything we do comes under the influence of prayer. We may choose to develop our awareness of God's presence, as a Father to us, with a few general prayers (p. 172) together with some morning prayers (p. 176). This may lead us into praise of God the Father (p. 19), to some devotion to Jesus our Savior (p. 36), or to imploring the help and guidance of the Holy Spirit (p. 65).

We may wish to pray for a particular need of our world and community (p. 224), for someone who is ill (p. 235), or for some spiritual need for ourselves (p. 239). We may desire to consecrate the day and our lives to God (p. 176) or to implore the assistance of Our Lady (p. 270), the angels, and the saints (p. 292). A favorite litany or a phrase from it, or any prayer that has a special significance for us, may help to put our day in focus so that our waking hours are shot through with the light of God's love.

If we have a few quiet moments during the day, then we can develop our spiritual awareness of God using the Jesus Psalter (p. 37), the Jesus Prayer (p. 214), the Devotion to the Five Sacred Wounds (p. 61), the Thirty Days Prayer (p. 276), the *Bona Mors* (p. 310), or some other devotion. Favorite Catholic devotions, like the Way of the Cross (p. 54) and the rosary (p. 280), have been of immense spiritual benefit in the lives of countless Catholics through the ages. Similarly litanies, novenas, and the prayers of the saints are parts of our treasure house of Catholic spirituality.

We are a sacramental people. The section on the sacraments, especially the Mass, includes many prayers hallowed throughout the ages as well as the updated Mass prayers from the 2011 *Roman Missal*. These plunge the Catholic ever deeper into the personal life of Christ in his surrender to the Father.

The Mass is the center of our lives. We can recall its power during the day by saying the prayers for before and after Mass (pp. 81, 127), those for before and after Communion (pp. 129, 135), and those to be prayed in the presence of the Blessed Sacrament (p. 139). We are aware of God's mercy to us in the sacrament of reconciliation (p. 159) and of our rebirth as Christians in the sacrament of baptism (p. 74). Finally, we have special prayers for the evening's close (p. 194) and prayers of the Spirit (p. 200).

The manner in which each person uses *The Catholic Prayer Book* will be unique as he or she grows in the life of the Spirit. That the reader will come to love and treasure this book as an instrument that leads to a fuller life with God: This is its function and my prayer for you.

Michael Buckley

From the very beginning God the Father intended Christ to be the crowning point and purpose of creation. "He is the image of the unseen God, the first-born of all creation" (Colossians 1:15). He is the center in which the human capacity for union with God is to be fully realized: "For in him all the fullness of God was pleased to dwell" (Colossians 1:19). We were to share the life of the Son and to come to the Father through him. We were to be sons of God and possess his Spirit. Such was God's purpose for us. This was our destiny.

However, God created man free. In his freedom man created a sin-filled history. Humanity became a fallen race. It needed to be redeemed and restored to its former destiny. It is into this sin-filled world that, "when the time had fully come, God sent forth his Son, born of woman, born under the law, to redeem those who were under the law, so that we might receive adoption as sons" (Galatians 4:4–5). Christ is the restorer of man's dignity and destiny.

The testimony of the Son to the Father, given the conditions of this fallen world, was manifested in his perfect obedience to his Father's will, even to death on a cross. The life and death of the Son reveal God the Father as a saving God whose love overcomes man's sinfulness: "God so loved the world that he gave his only-begotten Son, that whoever believes in him should not perish but have eternal life" (John 3:16). The Father responds to his Son's perfect love and obedience by raising him from the dead and setting him at his right hand in glory. The humiliated servant is revealed as the Lord of Glory whose destiny we now share.

In Christ a new age is established. He has conquered sin, death, and the world and has passed to his heavenly existence, where he awaits those who believe in him. He will come again at the final consummation of all things, and in him the fall and rise of creation will find their true meaning. As Christians we are a new creation. We are an Easter people whose praise of God is rooted in the Resurrection.

God's original plan of uniting all mankind to himself is now being fulfilled in Christ's Church, the community of believers. Just as the Father chose a people, the Israelites, to proclaim his presence and love in the world, so now the Church, Christ's body on earth, proclaims the loving fatherhood of God in his risen Son. To enable us to do this, Christ sends his Holy Spirit to us:

> All who are led by the Spirit of God are sons of God. For you did not receive the spirit of slavery to fall back into fear, but you have received the spirit of sonship. When we cry, "Abba! Father!" it is the Spirit himself bearing witness with our spirit that we are children of God. (Romans 8:14–16)

The Christian life is, therefore, the life of the Blessed Trinity. Created by the Father, redeemed by the Son, and sanctified by the Holy Spirit, we live out our destiny in the Church and the world through prayer and the sacraments. This is our Christian vocation.

## PRAYERS TO GOD THE FATHER

*God is our Father, to whom all prayer is directed. We were made to know, love, and serve him. Every gift comes from him as its source and returns to him as its final end. We praise and adore him for all the gifts of creation but especially for the gift of his only Son, by whom we are redeemed.*

### Prayers of Thanksgiving

#### *A General Thanksgiving*

Lord, open my lips, and my mouth shall proclaim your praise. To you be glory in the Church and in Christ Jesus from generation to generation evermore.

Almighty God of all mercies, Father,
we, your unworthy servants,
give you most humble and hearty thanks
for all your goodness and loving kindness
to us and to all men.

We bless you for our creation, our preservation,
and all the blessings of this life.

But above all we thank you for your infinite love
in the redemption of the world by our Lord Jesus Christ,
for the means of grace and the hope of glory.

And, we pray, give us a due sense of all your mercies,
that our hearts may be truly thankful
and that we may declare your praise
not only with our lips but in our lives,

by giving ourselves to your service
and by walking before you in holiness and righteousness all our days.

Through Jesus Christ our Lord,
to whom, with you and the Holy Spirit,
be all honor and glory world without end.

***Give Thanks to the Lord***

O give thanks to the LORD, for he is good,
  for his mercy endures for ever.
O give thanks to the God of gods,
  for his mercy endures for ever.
O give thanks to the Lord of lords,
  for his mercy endures for ever;
to him who alone does great wonders,
  for his mercy endures for ever;
to him who by understanding made the heavens,
  for his mercy endures for ever;
to him who spread out the earth upon the waters,
  for his mercy endures for ever;
to him who made the great lights,
  for his mercy endures for ever;
the sun to rule over the day,
  for his mercy endures for ever;
the moon and stars to rule over the night,
  for his mercy endures for ever;
...
He...gives food to all flesh,
for his mercy endures for ever

O give thanks to the God of heaven,
for his mercy endures for ever.

Psalm 136:1–9, 25–26

***Thanksgiving for Creation***

Thanks be to God for the light and the darkness;
Thanks be to God for the hail and the snow;
Thanks be to God for shower and sunshine;
Thanks be to God for all things that grow;
Thanks be to God for lightning and tempests;
Thanks be to God for weal and woe;
Thanks be to God for his own great goodness;
Thanks be to God for what is, is so;
Thanks be to God when the harvest is plenty;
Thanks be to God when the barn is low;
Thanks be to God when our pockets are empty;
Thanks be to God when again they o'erflow.

***Thanksgiving for Salvation***

He is the image of the unseen God
and the first-born of all creation,
for in him were created
all things in heaven and on earth:
everything visible and everything invisible,
Thrones, Dominations, Sovereignties, Powers—
all things were created through him and for him.
Before anything was created, he existed,
and he holds all things in unity.
Now the Church is his body,
he is its head.

As he is the Beginning,
he was first to be born from the dead,
so that he should be first in every way;
because God wanted all perfection
to be found in him
and all things to be reconciled through him
and for him,
everything in heaven and everything on earth,
when he made peace
by his death on the cross.

Colossians 1:15–20

***Thanksgiving for the Gift of Faith***

My God, from my heart I thank you for the many blessings you have given me. I thank you for having created and baptized me, for having placed me in your holy Catholic Church, and for having given me so many graces and mercies through the merits of Jesus Christ. I thank your Son Jesus for having died upon the cross that I might receive pardon for my sins and obtain my eternal salvation. I thank you for all your other mercies you have given me through Jesus Christ, Our Lord.

**Prayers of Praise**

***How Majestic Is Your Name***

O Lord, our Lord,
how majestic is your name in all the earth!

You whose glory above the heavens is chanted
by the mouth of babes and infants,

you have founded a bulwark because of your foes,
  to still the enemy and the avenger.

When I look at your heavens, the work of your fingers,
  the moon and the stars which you have established;
what is man that you are mindful of him,
  and the son of man that you care for him?

Yet you have made him little less than the angels,
  and you have crowned him with glory and honor.
You have given him dominion over the works of your hands;
  you have put all things under his feet,
all sheep and oxen,
  and also the beasts of the field,
the birds of the air, and the fish of the sea,
whatever passes along the paths of the sea.

O Lord, our Lord,
  how majestic is your name in all the earth!

Psalm 8

***Praise for All Creation***

I offer thee
Every flower that ever grew,
Every bird that ever flew,
Every wind that ever blew.
Good God!

Every thunder rolling,
Every church bell tolling,
Every leaf and sod.
*Laudamus Te!*

I offer thee
Every wave that ever moved,
Every heart that ever loved,
Thee, thy Father's well-beloved.
Dear Lord!

Every river dashing,
Every lightning flashing,
Like an angel's sword.
*Benedicimus Te!*

I offer thee
Every cloud that ever swept
O'er the skies, and broke and wept
In rain, and with the flowerets slept.
My King!

Every communicant praying,
Every angel staying
Before thy throne to sing.
*Adoramus Te!*

I offer thee
Every flake of virgin snow,
Every spring of earth below,
Every human joy and woe.
My love!

O Lord! And all thy glorious
Self o'er death victorious,

Throned in heaven above.
*Glorificamus Te!*

Ancient Irish Prayer

***Pied Beauty***

Glory be to God for dappled things—
For skies of couple-colour as a brinded cow;
For rose-moles all in stipple upon trout that swim;
Fresh-firecoal chestnut-falls; finches' wings;
Landscape plotted and pierced—fold, fallow, and plough;
And all trades, their gear and tackle and trim.

All things counter, original, spare, strange;
Whatever is fickle, freckled (who knows how?)
With swift, slow; sweet, sour; adazzle, dim;
He fathers-forth whose beauty is past change:
Praise him.

Gerard Manley Hopkins

***For the Beauty of the Earth***

For the beauty of the earth,
For the glory of the skies,
For the love which from our birth,
Over and around us lies:

Lord of all to Thee we raise
This our hymn of grateful praise.

For the wonder of each hour
Of the day and of the night,
Hill and vale and tree and flow'r,

Sun and moon and stars of light:

Lord of all to Thee we raise
This our hymn of grateful praise.

For the joy of human love,
Brother, sister, parent, child,
Friends on earth and friends above,
For all gentle thoughts and mild:

Lord of all to Thee we raise
This our hymn of grateful praise.

For Thy Church that evermore
Lifteth holy hands above,
Offering up on every shore
Her pure sacrifice of love

Lord of all to Thee we raise
This our hymn of grateful praise.

William C. Dix

***Hymn of Praise***
Most high Lord,
Yours are the praises,
The glory and the honors,
And to you alone must be accorded
All graciousness; and no man there is
Who is worthy to name you.
Be praised, O God, and be exalted,
My Lord of all creatures,

And in especial of the most high Sun,
Which is your creature, O Lord, that makes clear
The day and illumines it,
Whence by its fairness and its splendor
It is become your face;
And of the white moon (be praised, O Lord)
And of the wandering stars,
Created by you in the heaven
So brilliant and so fair.
Praised be my Lord, by the flame
Whereby night grows illumined
In the midst of its darkness,
For it is resplendent,
Is joyous, fair, eager; is mighty.
Praised be my Lord by the flame
Of the winds, of the clear sky,
And of the cloudy, praised
Of all seasons whereby
Live all these creatures
Of lower order.
Praised be my Lord,
By our sister the water,
Element meet for man,
Humble and chaste in its clearness.
Praised be the Lord by our mother
The Earth that sustains,
That feeds, that produces
Multitudinous grasses

And flowers and fruitage.
Praised be my Lord, by those
Who grant pardons through his love,
Enduring their travail in patience
And their infirmity with joy of the spirit.
Praised be my Lord by death corporal
Whence escapes no one living.
Woe to those that die in mutual transgression,
And blessed are they who shall
Find in death's hour your grace that comes
From obedience to your holy will,
Wherethrough they shall never see
The pain of the death eternal.
Praise and give grace to my Lord,
Be grateful and serve him
In humbleness even as you are.
Praise him, all creatures!

St. Francis of Assisi, translated by Ezra Pound*

***Psalms of Praise***

Praise the LORD!
Praise, O servants of the LORD,
praise the name of the LORD!

Blessed be the name of the LORD
from this time forth and for evermore!
From the rising of the sun to its setting
the name of the LORD is to be praised!

The Lord is high above all nations,
  and his glory above the heavens!

Who is like the Lord our God,
  who is seated on high,
who looks far down
  upon the heavens and the earth?
He raises the poor from the dust,
  and lifts the needy from the ash heap,
to make them sit with princes,
  with the princes of his people.
He gives the barren woman a home,
  making her the joyous mother of children.
Praise the Lord!

Psalm 113

Let the peoples praise you, O God;
  let all the peoples praise you!

Let the nations be glad and sing for joy,
  for you judge the peoples with equity
  and guide the nations upon earth.
Let the peoples praise you, O God;
  let all the peoples praise you!

The earth has yielded its increase;
  God, our God, has blessed us.
God has blessed us;
  let all the ends of the earth fear him!

Psalm 67:3–7

I give you thanks, O Lord,
with my whole heart;
before the angels I sing your praise;
I bow down toward your holy temple
and give thanks to your name for your mercy and your faithfulness;
for you have exalted above everything
your name and your word.
On the day I called, you answered me,
my strength of soul you increased.

All the kings of the earth shall praise you, O Lord,
for they have heard the words of your mouth;
and they shall sing of the ways of the Lord,
for great is the glory of the Lord.
For though the Lord is high, he regards the lowly;
but the haughty he knows from afar.

Though I walk in the midst of trouble,
you preserve my life;
you stretch out your hand against the wrath of my enemies,
and your right hand delivers me.
The Lord will fulfil his purpose for me;
your mercy, O Lord, endures for ever.
Do not forsake the work of your hands.

Psalm 138

I will extol you, O Lord, for you have drawn me up,
and have not let my foes rejoice over me.

O Lord my God, I cried to you for help,
and you have healed me.
O Lord, you have brought up my soul from Sheol,
restored me to life from among those gone down to the Pit.

Sing praises to the Lord, O you his saints,
and give thanks to his holy name.
For his anger is but for a moment,
and his favor is for a lifetime.
Weeping may last for the night,
but joy comes with the morning.

As for me, I said in my prosperity,
"I shall never be moved."
By your favor, O Lord,
you had established me as a strong mountain;
you hid your face,
I was dismayed.

To you, O Lord, I cried;
and to the Lord I made supplication:
"What profit is there in my death,
if I go down to the Pit?
Will the dust praise you?
Will it tell of your faithfulness?
Hear, O Lord, and be gracious to me!
O Lord, be my helper!"

You have turned my mourning into dancing;
you have loosed my sackcloth

and clothed me with gladness,
that my soul may praise you and not be silent.
O LORD my God, I will give thanks to you for ever.

Psalm 30

I will extol you, my God and King,
and bless your name for ever and ever.
Every day I will bless you,
and praise your name for ever and ever.
Great is the LORD, and greatly to be praised,
and his greatness is unsearchable.

One generation shall laud your works to another,
and shall declare your mighty acts.
On the glorious splendor of your majesty,
and on your wondrous works, I will meditate.
Men shall proclaim the might of your awesome acts,
and I will declare your greatness.
They shall pour forth the fame of your abundant goodness,
and shall sing aloud of your righteousness.

The LORD is gracious and merciful,
slow to anger and abounding in mercy.
The LORD is good to all,
and his compassion is over all that he has made.

All your works shall give thanks to you, O LORD,
and all your saints shall bless you!
They shall speak of the glory of your kingdom,
and tell of your power,

to make known to the sons of men your mighty deeds,
  and the glorious splendor of your kingdom.
Your kingdom is an everlasting kingdom,
  and your dominion endures throughout all generations.

The LORD is faithful in all his words,
  and gracious in all his deeds.
The LORD upholds all who are falling,
  and raises up all who are bowed down.
The eyes of all look to you,
  and you give them their food in due season.
You open your hand,
  you satisfy the desire of every living thing.
The LORD is just in all his ways,
  and kind in all his doings.
The LORD is near to all who call upon him,
  to all who call upon him in truth.
He fulfils the desire of all who fear him,
  he also hears their cry, and saves them.
The LORD preserves all who love him;
  but all the wicked he will destroy.

My mouth will speak the praise of the LORD,
  and let all flesh bless his holy name for ever and ever.

Psalm 145

***Pope John Paul II's Prayer of Praise***

God, you are our Creator.
You are good, and your mercy knows no bounds.

To you arises the praise of every creature.
God, you have given us an inner law by which we must live.
To do your will is our task.
To follow your ways is to know peace of heart.
To you we offer our homage.
Guide us on all the paths we travel upon this earth.
Free us from all the evil tendencies that lead our hearts away from your will.
Never allow us to stray from you.
O God, judge of all humankind, help us to be included among your chosen ones on the last day.
God, Author of peace and justice, give us true joy and authentic love, and a lasting solidarity among peoples.
Give us your everlasting gifts. Amen.

Pope John Paul II

***Magnificat***

My soul magnifies the Lord,
and my spirit rejoices in God my Savior,
for he has regarded the low estate of his handmaiden.
For behold, henceforth all generations will call me blessed;
for he who is mighty has done great things for me,
and holy is his name.
And his mercy is on those who fear him
from generation to generation.
He has shown strength with his arm,
he has scattered the proud in the imagination of their hearts,
he has put down the mighty from their thrones,
and exalted those of low degree;

he has filled the hungry with good things,
and the rich he has sent empty away.
He has helped his servant Israel,
in remembrance of his mercy,
as he spoke to our fathers,
to Abraham and to his posterity for ever.

Luke 1:46–55

***Praise to the Infinite God***

Infinite God, the brightness of whose face is often
hidden from my mortal gaze,
I thank you that you sent your Son,
Jesus Christ, to be a light in a dark world.
I thank you, Christ, light of light, that in your most holy life
you pierced the eternal mystery as with a great shaft of light,
so that on seeing you we see him whom no one has ever seen.

John Baillie*

***Lord of All Life***

Lord of all life, we praise you, that through Christ's resurrection, the old order of sin and death is overcome and all things made new in him: grant that being dead to sin we may live to you in newness of life through Jesus Christ, Our Lord.

## PRAYERS TO GOD THE SON

*Jesus came that we might share his risen life. He is one with the Father. The Christian life is a communion of love joining us with God and with each other. Christ is the center of the circle, the hourglass through which our lives flow in prayer in order to be purified from the effects of sin. All our prayer, by the power of his Spirit, is directed to the Father through Christ's risen life at work in us. We are a resurrection people, and "alleluia" is our song.*

***Praise to the Holiest in the Height***

Praise to the holiest in the height,
And in the depth be praise:
In all his words most wonderful;
Most sure in all his ways!

O loving wisdom of our God!
When all was sin and shame,
A second Adam to the fight
And to the rescue came.

O wisest love! that flesh and blood
Which did in Adam fail,
Should strive afresh against the foe,
Should strive and should prevail.

And that a higher gift than grace
Should flesh and blood refine,
God's presence and his very self,
And essence all divine.

O generous love! that he who smote
In man for man the foe,
The double agony in man
For man should undergo;

And in the garden secretly,
And on the cross on high,
Should teach his brethren and inspire
To suffer and to die.

St. John Henry Newman

***The Jesus Psalter***

*The Psalter is made up of three parts, each part consisting of five petitions. Each petition is followed by the prayers* "Have mercy on all sinners, Jesus, I beseech you…" *and* "O blessed Trinity…" *The fifth, tenth, and fifteenth petitions, which bring the three parts to a close, conclude with* "He was humbler yet…," "Hear these my petitions…," *and* "I believe in God…"

PART ONE

*Begin by kneeling devoutly, or bowing, at the adorable name of JESUS, saying:*

At the name of Jesus every knee should bow,
in heaven and on earth and under the earth,
and every tongue confess that Jesus Christ is Lord,
to the glory of God the Father.

Philippians 2:10–11

*First Petition*

Jesus, Jesus, Jesus,
Jesus, Jesus, Jesus, have mercy on me.
Jesus, Jesus, Jesus,

Jesus, have mercy on me, O God of compassion, and forgive the many and great offenses that I have committed in your sight.

Many have been the follies of my life, and great are the miseries I have deserved for my ingratitude.

Have mercy on me, dear Jesus, for I am weak;

O Lord, heal me, who am unable to help myself.

Deliver me from setting my heart upon any of your creatures, which may divert my eyes from a continual looking up to you.

Grant me grace henceforth, for the love of you, to hate sin; and out of a just esteem of you, to despise all worldly vanities.

Have mercy on all sinners, Jesus, I beseech you; turn their vices into virtues; and making them true observers of your law and sincere lovers of you, bring them to bliss in everlasting glory.

Have mercy also on the souls in purgatory, for your bitter passion, I beseech you, and for your glorious name, Jesus.

O blessed Trinity, one eternal God, have mercy on me.

Our Father. Hail Mary.

*Second Petition*

Jesus, Jesus, Jesus,
Jesus, Jesus, Jesus, have mercy on me.
Jesus, Jesus, Jesus,

Jesus, help me to overcome all temptations to sin and the malice of my spiritual enemy.
Help me to spend my time in virtuous actions and in such labors as are acceptable to you.
Help me to resist and repel the inclinations of my flesh to sloth, gluttony, and impurity.
Help me to make my heart be attracted by virtue and inflamed with desires of your glorious presence.
Help me to deserve and keep a good name, by a peaceful and holy living; to your honor, O Jesus, to my own peace and the benefit of others.
Have mercy on all sinners,... O blessed Trinity,...
Our Father. Hail Mary.

*Third Petition*
Jesus, Jesus, Jesus,
Jesus, Jesus, Jesus, strengthen me.
Jesus, Jesus, Jesus,
Jesus, strengthen me in soul and body, to please you in doing such works of virtue as may bring me to your everlasting joy and happiness.
Grant me a firm purpose, most merciful Savior, to amend my life and to compensate for the years past:
Those years that I have misspent in vain or wicked thoughts, words, deeds, and evil habits.
Make my heart obedient to your will and ready, for your love, to perform all the works of mercy.
Grant me the gifts of the Holy Spirit, which by a virtuous life and devout frequenting of your most holy sacraments, will

bring me to your heavenly kingdom.
Have mercy on all sinners,...O blessed Trinity,...
Our Father. Hail Mary.

*Fourth Petition*

Jesus, Jesus, Jesus,
Jesus, Jesus, Jesus, comfort me.
Jesus, Jesus, Jesus,
Jesus, comfort me, and give me grace to place my chief, my only joy and happiness in you.
Give me the grace of contemplative prayer, inner peace, and a fervent desire of your glory; fill my soul with the contemplation of heaven, that I may dwell there everlastingly with you.
Bring often to my remembrance your unsurpassable goodness, your gifts, and the great kindness you have shown me.
And when you bring to my mind the sad remembrance of my sins, whereby I have so ungratefully offended you, comfort me with the assurance of obtaining your grace by the spirit of perfect repentance, which will take away my guilt and prepare me for your kingdom.
Have mercy on all sinners,...O blessed Trinity,...
Our Father. Hail Mary.

*Fifth Petition*

Jesus, Jesus, Jesus,
Jesus, Jesus, Jesus, make me constant.
Jesus, Jesus, Jesus,
Jesus, make me constant in faith, hope, and charity; and give

me perseverance in all virtues and a resolution never to offend you.
Let the memory of your passion, and of those bitter pains you suffered for me, strengthen my patience and defend me in all tribulation and adversity.
Let me always hold fast to the doctrines of your Catholic Church and fulfill all my Christian obligations.
Let no false delight of this deceitful world blind me, no temptation of the flesh or fraud of the devil shake my heart: my heart, which seeks you for its eternal rest and resolves to seek your eternal reward above all else.
Have mercy on all sinners,… O blessed Trinity,…
He humbled himself and became obedient unto death, even death on a cross.

Philippians 2:8

Hear these my petitions, O most merciful Savior, and grant me grace to repeat and consider them frequently so that they may prove easy steps whereby my soul may ascend to the knowledge, love, and performance of my duty to you and my neighbor, through the whole course of my life. Amen.
Our Father. Hail Mary.
I believe in God,…

PART TWO

*Begin as for Part One, kneeling devoutly or bowing at the adorable name of JESUS, saying:*

At the name of Jesus every knee should bow,
in heaven and on earth and under the earth,
and every tongue confess that Jesus Christ is Lord,
to the glory of God the Father.

Philippians 2:10–11

*Sixth Petition*

Jesus, Jesus, Jesus,
Jesus, Jesus, Jesus, enlighten me with spiritual wisdom.
Jesus, Jesus, Jesus,

Jesus, enlighten me with spiritual wisdom to know your goodness and all those things that are most acceptable to you. Grant me a clear understanding of my only good, and wisdom to order my life according to it.

Grant that I may grow in virtue, till at length I arrive at the clear vision of your glorious majesty.

Permit me not, dear Lord, to return to those sins for which I have been sorry, and which I have confessed and done penance for.

Grant me grace to benefit the souls of others by my good example and to win back, by good counsel, those who offend against me.

Have mercy on all sinners,…O blessed Trinity,…

Our Father. Hail Mary.

*Seventh Petition*

Jesus, Jesus, Jesus,
Jesus, Jesus, Jesus, grant me grace to fear you.
Jesus, Jesus, Jesus,

Jesus, grant me grace inwardly to fear losing your friendship and to avoid all occasions of offending you.
Let your warning of the punishments that are to fall on sinners, the fear of losing your love and your heavenly inheritance, always keep me in awe.
Let me not risk losing your friendship by sin but soon return to repentance, lest the sentence of endless death and damnation fall upon me.
Let the powerful intercession of your Blessed Mother and all your saints, but above all, your own merits and mercy, O my Savior, be ever between your righteous justice and my soul still tempted by sin.
Enable me, O my God, to work out my salvation with fear and trembling; and let the understanding of your secret judgments render me a more humble and diligent lover at the throne of your grace.
Have mercy on all sinners,… O blessed Trinity,…
Our Father. Hail Mary.

*Eighth Petition*
Jesus, Jesus, Jesus,
Jesus, Jesus, Jesus, grant me grace to love you.
Jesus, Jesus, Jesus,
Jesus, grant me grace truly to love you for your infinite goodness and for the wonderful bounties I have received and hope for ever to receive from you.
Let the remembrance of your kindness and patience conquer the malice and wretched inclinations of my fallen nature.
Let the consideration of my many deliverances, your frequent

graces, and continual assistance in my life make me ashamed of my ingratitude.

You grant me all your mercies, so that I may love you as my only good.

O my dear Lord, my whole life shall be nothing but a desire of you; and because I indeed love you, I will most lovingly keep your commandments.

Have mercy on all sinners,... O blessed Trinity,...

Our Father. Hail Mary.

*Ninth Petition*

Jesus, Jesus, Jesus,
Jesus, Jesus, Jesus, grant me grace to remember my
Jesus, Jesus, Jesus, death.

Jesus, grant me grace always to remember my death and the account that I am then to give, so that my soul, being always well disposed, may depart out of this world in your grace.

Then, by the holy intercession of your Blessed Mother and St. Joseph and the assistance of the glorious St. Michael, deliver me from the enemy of my soul; and do you, my good angel, I beseech you, help me at that most solemn hour.

Then, dear Jesus, remember your mercy, and turn not your most lovable face away from me because of my offenses.

Prepare me for that day, by causing me now to die daily to all earthly things and so to have my conversation continually in heaven.

Let the remembrance of my death teach me how to esteem my life, and the memory of your resurrection encourage me to meet my death with cheerfulness.

Have mercy on all sinners,… O blessed Trinity,…
Our Father. Hail Mary.

*Tenth Petition*

Jesus, Jesus, Jesus,
Jesus, Jesus, Jesus, send me here my purgatory
Jesus, Jesus, Jesus,
Jesus, send me here my purgatory, so that I may be made ready to share the happiness of heaven. Grant me those merciful crosses and afflictions that take away my false affection for all things here below.
Since no one can see you that loves anything that is not for your sake, suffer not my heart to find any rest here but in you alone.
Grant that I may never suffer from the anguish of a soul that is separated from you, the soul that desires you but cannot come to you because of sin.
Keep me continually mortified to this world, that being thoroughly purified by the fire of your love, I may immediately pass from this life into your everlasting kingdom.
Have mercy on all sinners,… O blessed Trinity,…
He humbled himself and became obedient unto death, even death on a cross.

Philippians 2:8

Hear these my petitions, O my most merciful Savior, and grant me grace to repeat and consider them frequently so that they may prove easy steps whereby my soul may ascend to the knowledge, love, and performance of my duty to you and my

neighbor, through the whole course of my life. Amen.
Our Father. Hail Mary.
I believe in God,...

PART THREE

*Begin as for Part One, kneeling devoutly or bowing at the adorable name of JESUS, saying:*

At the name of Jesus every knee should bow,
in heaven and on earth and under the earth,
and every tongue confess that Jesus Christ is Lord,
to the glory of God the Father.

Philippians 2:10–11

*Eleventh Petition*

Jesus, Jesus, Jesus,
Jesus, Jesus, Jesus, help me in my human relationships.
Jesus, Jesus, Jesus,

Jesus, help me in my human relationships, so that I may always see you in the other person.

Cause me, O blessed Lord, to remember always that you are present to all our words and actions. May I always speak the truth in charity and never hurt my neighbor by speaking evil of him when it is better to be silent.

Control in me, dear Jesus, all inordinate affections to things of the flesh, so that I treat other people with love and respect.

Your power defend, your wisdom direct, your fatherly pity correct me, and make me so live here among people that I may be fit for the conversation of angels hereafter.

Have mercy on all sinners,… O blessed Trinity,…
Our Father. Hail Mary.

*Twelfth Petition*

Jesus, Jesus, Jesus,
Jesus, Jesus, Jesus, grant me grace to call on you for
Jesus, Jesus, Jesus, help.

Jesus, grant me grace in all my needs to call on you for help, faithfully remembering your death and resurrection for my sake.

You will listen to my cries because you laid down your life for my ransom, and you will save me because you took it up again for your crown.

You intercede for me in heaven because you have promised: "Call upon me in the day of trouble: I will deliver you" (Psalm 50:15).

You are my sure rock of defense against all sorts of enemies; you are my ever-present grace, able to strengthen me to every good work.

Therefore, in all my sufferings, weaknesses, and temptations, I will confidently call on you; hear me, O my Jesus, and when you hear, have mercy.

Have mercy on all sinners,… O blessed Trinity,…
Our Father. Hail Mary.

*Thirteenth Petition*

Jesus, Jesus, Jesus,
Jesus, Jesus, Jesus, make me persevere in virtue.
Jesus, Jesus, Jesus

Jesus, make me persevere in virtue and a good life, and may I never fail in your service, till you bring me to my place in your kingdom.

In every aspect of my work and prayer, strengthen, O Lord, my soul and body. May I see life as a pilgrimage on earth toward the new Jerusalem, a journey I must constantly pursue without turning from the true path. O Jesus, make me always consider your blessed example: through how much pain you pressed on to a bitter death, your way to a glorious resurrection.

Make me, O my Redeemer, seriously weigh your words, "He who endures to the end will be saved" (Matthew 24:13).

Have mercy on all sinners,… O blessed Trinity,…

Our Father. Hail Mary.

*Fourteenth Petition*

Jesus, Jesus, Jesus,
Jesus, Jesus, Jesus, grant me grace to fix my mind on
Jesus, Jesus, Jesus, you.

Jesus, grant me grace to fix my mind on you, especially in time of prayer, when I directly converse with you.

Stop the wanderings of my mind and the desires of my fickle heart; suppress the power of my spiritual enemies, who endeavor at that time to draw me from thinking of and loving you.

So shall I, with joy and gratitude, look on you as my deliverer from all the evils I have escaped and as my benefactor for all the good I have ever received or can hope for.
I shall see that you are my only good and that all other things are but means, ordained by you, to make me fix my mind on you, to make me love you more and more, and by loving you, to be eternally happy.
O beloved of my soul, sanctify all my thoughts on earth, that my eyes may become worthy to behold you face-to-face in your glory for ever.
Have mercy on all sinners,… O blessed Trinity,…
Our Father. Hail Mary.

*Fifteenth Petition*

Jesus, Jesus, Jesus,
Jesus, Jesus, Jesus, give me grace to order my life
Jesus, Jesus, Jesus, toward my eternal happiness.

Jesus, give me grace to order my life toward my eternal happiness; so that all the actions of my body and soul may fit me for eternal happiness with you.
May I see this world as a place in which we live in order to fit us for the next by desiring God as our only end.
Break my proud spirit, O Jesus; make it humble and obedient: Grant me grace to depart this life with a heart filled with joy at my going to you.
Let the memory of your passion make me cheerfully undergo all temptations or sufferings here for your love, while my soul

longs for that blissful life and immortal glory, which you have prepared in heaven for your servants.

O Jesus, let me frequently and attentively consider that whatever I gain, if I lose you, all is lost; and whatever I lose, if I gain you, all is gained.

Have mercy on all sinners,… O blessed Trinity,…

He humbled himself and became obedient unto death, even death on a cross.

Philippians 2:8

Hear these my petitions, O my most merciful Savior, and grant me grace so frequently to repeat and consider them that they may prove easy steps whereby my soul may ascend to the knowledge, love, and performance of my duty to you and my neighbor, through the whole course of my life. Amen.

Our Father. Hail Mary.

I believe in God,…

***The Litany of the Sacred Heart***

Lord, have mercy on us.

Lord, have mercy on us.

Christ, have mercy on us.

Christ, have mercy on us.

Lord, have mercy on us.

Lord, have mercy on us.

Christ, hear us.

Christ, graciously hear us.

God the Father of heaven,

have mercy on us.

God the Son, redeemer of the world,

have mercy on us.

God the Holy Spirit,

have mercy on us.

Holy Trinity, one God,

have mercy on us.

Heart of Jesus, Son of the eternal Father,

have mercy on us.

Heart of Jesus, formed by the Holy Spirit in the womb of the virgin mother,

have mercy on us.

Heart of Jesus, wonderfully united to the eternal Word,

have mercy on us.

Heart of Jesus, of infinite majesty,

have mercy on us.

Heart of Jesus, holy temple of God,

have mercy on us.

Heart of Jesus, tabernacle of the Most High,

have mercy on us.

Heart of Jesus, house of God and gate of heaven,

have mercy on us.

Heart of Jesus, burning furnace of charity,

have mercy on us.

Heart of Jesus, vessel of justice and love,

have mercy on us.

Heart of Jesus, never-ending source of all virtues,

have mercy on us.

Heart of Jesus, worthy of all praise,
have mercy on us.
Heart of Jesus, king and center of all hearts,
have mercy on us.
Heart of Jesus, in which are all the treasures of wisdom and knowledge,
have mercy on us
Heart of Jesus, in which dwells all the fullness of the divinity,
have mercy on us.
Heart of Jesus, in which the Father is well pleased,
have mercy on us.
Heart of Jesus, of whose fullness we have all received,
have mercy on us.
Heart of Jesus, deepest desire of the human heart,
have mercy on us.
Heart of Jesus, patient and abounding in mercy,
have mercy on us.
Heart of Jesus, generous to all who call upon you,
have mercy on us
Heart of Jesus, fountain of life and holiness,
have mercy on us.
Heart of Jesus, atonement for our sins,
have mercy on us.
Heart of Jesus, which suffered rejection for our sake,
have mercy on us.
Heart of Jesus, bruised for our sins,
have mercy on us.

Heart of Jesus, made obedient unto death,
have mercy on us.
Heart of Jesus, pierced with a lance,
have mercy on us.
Heart of Jesus, source of all consolation,
have mercy on us.
Heart of Jesus, our peace and reconciliation,
have mercy on us.
Heart of Jesus, victim of our sins,
have mercy on us.
Heart of Jesus, salvation of those who hope in you,
have mercy on us.
Heart of Jesus, hope of those who die in you,
have mercy on us.
Heart of Jesus, our light and resurrection,
have mercy on us.
Heart of Jesus, delight of all the saints,
have mercy on us.
Lamb of God, you take away the sins of the world,
spare us, O Lord.
Lamb of God, you take away the sins of the world,
graciously hear us, O Lord.
Lamb of God, you take away the sins of the world,
have mercy on us.
Jesus, meek and humble of heart,
make our hearts like unto yours.

Let us pray.

Almighty and eternal God, look upon the heart of your

well-loved Son and the praises and sacrifice he offers you in the name of sinners; being pleased with his holy obedience, pardon those who implore your mercy and give us a share in his resurrection, in the name of the same Jesus Christ your Son, who lives and reigns with you in the unity of the Holy Spirit, one God for ever and ever.

Amen.

## *The Way of the Cross*

### PRAYER BEFORE THE WAY

Jesus Christ, my Lord, with what great love you passed over the painful road that led you to death; and I, how often have I abandoned you. But now I love you with my whole soul, and because I love you, I am sincerely sorry for having offended you. My Jesus, pardon me, and permit me to accompany you in this journey. You are going to die for love of me, and it is my wish also, my dearest Redeemer, to die for love of you. Jesus, in your love I wish to live; in your love I wish to die.

*First Station: Jesus Is Condemned to Death*

*This response is said before each station:*

**We adore you, Christ, and praise you.**

**Because by your holy cross you have redeemed the world.**

Consider how Jesus, after having been scourged and crowned with thorns, was unjustly condemned by Pilate to die on the cross.

My loving Jesus, it was not Pilate; no, it was my sins that condemned you to die. I beseech you, by the merits of this sorrowful journey, to assist my soul in her journey toward eternity.

*The following prayers and verse are said at the end of each station.*

I love you, Jesus, my love, above all things;
I repent with my whole heart for having offended you.
Never permit me to separate myself from you again.
Grant that I may love you always,
then do with me what you will.
Our Father. Hail Mary. Glory Be to the Father.

*Second Station: Jesus Receives the Cross*

**We adore...**

Consider how Jesus, in making this journey with the cross on his shoulders, thought of us, and offered for us to his Father the death he was about to undergo.

My most beloved Jesus, I embrace all the tribulations you have destined for me until death. I beseech you, by the merits of the pain you suffered in carrying your cross, to give me the necessary help to carry mine with perfect patience and resignation.

I love you, Jesus...Our Father. Hail Mary. Glory Be.

*Third Station: Jesus Falls the First Time*

**We adore...**

Consider the first fall of Jesus under his cross. His flesh was torn by the scourges; his head was crowned with thorns; he had lost a great quantity of blood. So weakened he could scarcely walk, he yet had to carry this great load upon his shoulders. The soldiers struck him rudely, and he fell several times.

My Jesus, it is not the weight of the cross but that of my sins that has made you suffer so much pain. By the merits of this first fall, deliver me from the misfortune of falling into mortal sin.
I love you, Jesus… Our Father. Hail Mary. Glory Be.

*Fourth Station: Jesus Meets His Blessed Mother*

**We adore…**

Consider the meeting of the Son and the mother that took place on this journey. Their looks became like so many arrows to wound those hearts that loved each other so tenderly.

My sweet Jesus, by the sorrow you experienced in this meeting, grant me the grace of a truly devoted love for your most holy mother. And you, my queen, overwhelmed with sorrow, obtain for me by your intercession a continual and tender remembrance of the passion of your Son.
I love you, Jesus… Our Father. Hail Mary. Glory Be.

*Fifth Station: Simon of Cyrene Helps Jesus Carry His Cross*

**We adore…**

Consider how his cruel tormentors, seeing Jesus was at the point of expiring and fearing he would die on the way rather than die the shameful death of the cross that they wished for him, constrained Simon of Cyrene to carry the cross behind our Lord.

My most beloved Jesus, I will not refuse the cross as the Cyrenian did: I accept it, I embrace it. I accept in particular the death you have destined for me, with all the pains that

may accompany it; I unite it to your death; I offer it to you. You died for love of me; I will die for love of you. Help me by your grace.
I love you, Jesus… Our Father. Hail Mary. Glory Be.

*Sixth Station: Veronica Wipes the Face of Jesus*

**We adore…**

Consider how the holy woman named Veronica, seeing Jesus so ill-used and his face bathed in sweat and blood, presented him with a towel, with which he wiped his adorable face, leaving on it the impression of his holy countenance.

My most beloved Jesus, your face was beautiful before; but in this journey it has lost all its beauty, and wounds and blood have disfigured it. My soul also was once beautiful, when it received your grace in baptism; but I have disfigured it since by my sins. You alone, my Redeemer, by your passion, can restore it to its former beauty.
I love you, Jesus… Our Father. Hail Mary. Glory Be.

*Seventh Station: Jesus Falls the Second Time*

**We adore…**

Consider the second fall of Jesus under the cross, a fall that renews the pain of all the wounds in his head and members.

My most sweet Jesus, how many times have you pardoned me, and how many times have I fallen again and begun again to offend you. By the merits of this second fall, give me the necessary help to persevere in your grace until death. Grant

that in all temptations that assail me, I may always commend myself to you.
I love you, Jesus… Our Father. Hail Mary. Glory Be.

*Eighth Station: The Women of Jerusalem Mourn for Our Lord*

**We adore…**

Consider how these women wept with compassion at seeing Jesus in such a pitiable state, streaming with blood as he walked along. "Daughters of Jerusalem," said he, "do not weep for me, but weep for yourselves and for your children" (Luke 23:28).

My Jesus, laden with sorrows, I weep for the offenses I have committed against you, because of the pains they have deserved and still more because of the displeasure they have caused you, who has loved me so much. It is your love more than the fear of hell that causes me to weep for my sins.
I love you, Jesus… Our Father. Hail Mary. Glory Be.

*Ninth Station: Jesus Falls the Third Time*

**We adore…**

Consider the third fall of Jesus Christ. His weakness was extreme, and the cruelty of his executioners excessive as they tried to hasten his steps when he could scarcely move.

My loving Jesus, by the merits of the weakness you suffered in going to Calvary, give me strength sufficient to conquer all human respect and all my wicked passions, which have led me to reject your friendship.
I love you, Jesus… Our Father. Hail Mary. Glory Be.

*Tenth Station: Jesus Is Stripped of His Garments*

**We adore…**

Consider the violence with which Jesus was stripped by the executioners. His inner garments adhered to his torn flesh, and the soldiers dragged them off so roughly that the skin came with them. Take pity on your Savior thus cruelly treated.

My innocent Jesus, by the merits of the torments you felt, help me to strip myself of all affection for things of earth, in order that I may place all my love in you, who are so worthy of my love.

I love you, Jesus… Our Father. Hail Mary. Glory Be.

*Eleventh Station: Jesus Is Nailed to the Cross*

**We adore…**

Consider how Jesus, having been placed upon the cross, extended his hands and offered to his eternal Father the sacrifice of his life for our salvation. Those barbarians fastened him with nails and then, securing the cross, allowed him to die with anguish on this infamous gibbet.

My Jesus, loaded with contempt, nail my heart to your feet, that it may ever remain there to love you and never quit you again.

I love you, Jesus… Our Father. Hail Mary. Glory Be.

*Twelfth Station: Jesus Dies on the Cross*

**We adore…**

Consider how Jesus, being consumed with anguish

after three hours' agony on the cross, abandoned himself to the weight of his body, bowed his head, and died.

My dying Jesus, I kiss devoutly the cross on which you died for love of me. I have merited by my sins to die a miserable death. But your death is my hope. By the merits of your death, give me grace to die embracing your feet and burning with love for you. I commit my soul into your hands.

I love you, Jesus… Our Father. Hail Mary. Glory Be.

*Thirteenth Station: Jesus Is Taken Down From the Cross*

**We adore…**

Consider how, after our Lord had expired, two of his disciples, Joseph and Nicodemus, took him down from the cross and placed him in the arms of his afflicted mother, who received him with unutterable tenderness and pressed him to her bosom.

Mother of sorrow, for the love of this Son, accept me for your servant, and pray for me. And my Redeemer, since you have died for me, permit me to love you; for I wish but you and nothing more.

I love you, Jesus… Our Father. Hail Mary. Glory Be.

*Fourteenth Station: Jesus Is Placed in the Tomb*

**We adore…**

Consider how the disciples carried the body of Jesus to bury it. Accompanied by his holy mother, who arranged it in the sepulcher with her own hands, they then closed the tomb, and all withdrew

My buried Jesus, I kiss the stone that encloses you. But you rose again on the third day. I beseech you by your resurrection, make me rise glorious with you at the last day, to be always united with you in heaven, to praise you and love you for ever.
I love you, Jesus… Our Father. Hail Mary. Glory Be.

Let us pray.
Lord Jesus Christ, you walked the way to Calvary to rescue us from our sin, but the Father, pleased with your obedient submission to his will, glorified you in the Resurrection. May we follow obediently in your footsteps, so that one day we may share in the glory of your risen life. We make this prayer through you who lives with the Father and Holy Spirit, one God for ever and ever. Amen.

***Devotion to the Five Sacred Wounds***

Lord Jesus Christ, we adore the sacred wound of your left foot. We thank you for the pain that you endured with so much love and charity. We suffer with you in your sufferings, and we humbly beg pardon for our sins, which we deplore beyond all else. Convert all sinners, and make them understand the enormity of rejecting your love.
Jesus, hear us.
**Jesus, graciously hear us.**

Lord Jesus Christ, we adore the sacred wound of your right foot. We thank you for the pain that you endured with so much love and charity. We suffer with you in your sufferings, and we pray that you would grant us strength against all

temptations and prompt obedience in doing your holy will. Comfort, O Jesus, the poor, the miserable, the afflicted, and all who are tempted or persecuted. Most Just Judge, govern those who administer justice, and assist all those who labor in the care of souls.
Jesus, hear us.

**Jesus, graciously hear us.**

Lord Jesus Christ, we adore the sacred wound of your left hand. We thank you for the pain that you endured with so much love and charity. We suffer with you in your sufferings, and we pray that you would give us the grace to earnestly desire heaven. Grant us patience in all the trials of this life and conformity in all things to your blessed will. Pardon all our enemies and all those who bear ill will against us. Grant patience to the sick, and restore them to health; support with your grace all who are in their agony, that they may soon see your face in glory.
Jesus, hear us.

**Jesus, graciously hear us.**

Lord Jesus Christ, we adore the sacred wound of your right hand. We thank you for the pain that you endured with so much love and charity. We suffer with you in your sufferings, and we pray that you would grant us a resolute will to seek those things that are a help to our salvation. Grant us the grace of final perseverance, give your peace and relief to the souls in purgatory, and daily lead nearer to true holiness your servants in this world.

Jesus, hear us.

**Jesus, graciously hear us.**

Lord Jesus Christ, we adore the sacred wound in your blessed side. We thank you for the infinite love manifested toward us at the opening of your Sacred Heart. Grant us a pure and perfect charity, that we may love all things for your sake and you above all things. May we breathe our last in the presence of your divine love. Protect your holy Catholic Church, direct your vicar upon earth, bishops, priests, and all who labor for the sake of the gospel. Preserve in your holy service all Christian kings and rulers. Bring back into the way of salvation all those who have gone astray, and bring under your sacred will all the enemies of your holy name.

Jesus, hear us.

**Jesus, graciously hear us.**

Let us pray.

Lord Jesus Christ, we honor the five wounds that in your love you endured for us your servants, whom you have redeemed with your precious blood. Grant that our devotion to these wounds may console us with the thought that one day, through the power of your resurrection, we will be with you in paradise. We make this prayer to the Father, who with you and the Holy Spirit lives and reigns, God, for ever and ever.

**Amen.**

***Signs of Sorrow and Love***

I kiss the wounds in your sacred head,
with sorrow deep and true,

may every thought of mine this day
be an act of love for you.

I kiss the wounds in your sacred hands,
with sorrow deep and true,
may every touch of my hands this day
be an act of love for you.

I kiss the wounds in your sacred feet,
with sorrow deep and true,
may every step I take this day
be an act of love for you.

I kiss the wound in your sacred side,
with sorrow deep and true,
may every beat of my heart this day
be an act of love for you.

## PRAYERS TO THE HOLY SPIRIT

*The Holy Spirit is the gift of the risen Christ and his loving Father. Through him we pray to the Father and share in the fruits of the passion, death, and resurrection of Jesus Christ. The Holy Spirit is the inspirer of all prayer. He is united with us in every thought, word, and action that we offer to the Father, so that the life of the risen Christ is always at work in us through his inspiration.*

### For the Presence of the Holy Spirit

***Come, Holy Spirit***

Come, Holy Spirit, fill the hearts of your faithful,
and enkindle in them the fire of your love.
Send forth your Spirit, and they shall be created.
And you shall renew the face of the earth.
Let us pray.
O God, who has taught the hearts of the faithful by the light of the Holy Spirit, grant that by the gift of the same Spirit, we may be always truly wise and ever rejoice in his consolation. Amen.

***Come, Holy Ghost***

Come, Holy Ghost, Creator, come
from thy bright heavenly throne,
come, take possession of our souls,
and make them all thine own.

Thou who art called the Paraclete,
best gift of God above,

the living spring, the living fire,
sweet unction and true love.

Thou who art sev'nfold in thy grace,
finger of God's right hand;
his promise, teaching little ones
to speak and understand.

O guide our minds with thy blest light,
with love our hearts inflame;
and with thy strength, which ne'er decays,
confirm our mortal flame.

Far from us drive our deadly foe;
true peace unto us bring;
and through all perils lead us safe
beneath thy sacred wing.

Through thee may we the Father know,
through thee th'eternal Son,
and thee the Spirit of them both,
thrice-blessed Three in One.

All glory to the Father be,
with his co-equal Son;
same to thee, great Paraclete,
while endless ages run.

Ascribed to Rabanus Maurus

***Come, O Love Divine***
Come down, O love divine,
seek thou this soul of mine,

and visit it with thine own
ardor glowing;
O comforter, draw near,
within my heart appear
and kindle it, thy holy
flame bestowing.

O let it freely burn,
till earthly passions turn
to dust and ashes
in its heat consuming;
and let thy glorious light
shine ever on my sight
and clothe me round, the while my
path illuming.

Let holy charity
mine outward vesture be,
and lowliness become mine
inner clothing;
true lowliness of heart,
which takes the humbler part,
and o'er its own shortcomings
weeps with loathing.

And so the yearning strong,
with which the soul will long,
shall far outpass the power of
human telling;
for none can guess its grace,

till he become the place
wherein the Holy Spirit
makes his dwelling.

Bianco da Siena

***Come Cleanse Our Hearts***

O God, to whom all hearts are open, all hearts known, and from whom no secrets are hidden, cleanse the thoughts of our hearts by the inpouring of your Holy Spirit, that every thought and word of ours may begin from you, and in you be perfectly completed, through Christ our Lord.

***Come and Make Us Open***

Holy Spirit, come into our lives.

| | |
|---|---|
| Open our ears | to hear what you are saying to us in the things that happen to us in the people we meet |
| Open our eyes | to see the needs of the people around us. |
| Open our hands | to do our work well<br>to help when help is needed. |
| Open our lips | to tell others the good news of Jesus and bring comfort, happiness, and laughter to other people. |
| Open our minds | to discover new truth about you and the world. |
| Open our hearts | to love you and our fellow men as you have loved us in Jesus. |

To you, with our Father and the Son, one God, all honor and praise shall be given now and for ever.

### *A Prayer for Awakening*

Holy Spirit, come like a mighty rushing wind and awaken us out of our complacency, our apathy, our indifference. Disturb us, for we are too content to let things go on as they are and to let people go on not knowing you. Penetrate the closed gates of our hearts and make us live again. O Holy Spirit, create among us a mighty Christian revolution, and cast the fear of the unknown out of our lives.

Michael Hollings and Etta Gullick*

### *Spirit of the Living God*

Spirit of the living God,
 fall afresh on me.
Spirit of the living God,
 fall afresh on me.
Melt me, mold me,
 fill me, use me.
Spirit of the living God,
 fall afresh on me.

Spirit of the living God,
 fall afresh on us.
Spirit of the living God
 fall afresh on us.
Melt us, mold us,
 fill us, use us.
Spirit of the living God,
 fall afresh on us.

Michael Iverson

**For the Gifts of the Holy Spirit**

***Spirit of God, Send Your Gifts***

Spirit of wisdom, preside over all my thoughts, words and actions,
from this hour till the moment of my death.
Spirit of understanding, enlighten and teach me.
Spirit of counsel, direct my experience.
Spirit of fortitude, strengthen my weakness.
Spirit of knowledge, instruct my ignorance.
Spirit of piety, make me fervent in good works. Spirit of fear, restrain me from all evil. Spirit of peace, give me your peace.
Heavenly Spirit, make me persevere in the service of God the Father,
and enable me to act on all occasions with goodness, patience, charity, joy, generosity, mildness, and fidelity. Let the heavenly virtues of modesty, continence and chastity adorn the temple you have chosen for your abode, and by your all-powerful grace, preserve my soul from the misfortune of sin.

***Sanctify My Day***

Holy Spirit, as I awake and day begins,
waken me to your presence;
waken me to your indwelling;
waken me to inward sight of you,
and speech with you,
and strength from you;

that all my earthly walk may awaken into song
and my spirit leap up to you all day,
all ways.

Eric Milner-White*

***Set Us Ablaze***

Lord, no eye has seen, no ear has heard, no heart has conceived the things you have prepared for those who love you. Set us ablaze with the fire of the Holy Spirit, that we may love you in and above all things and so receive the rewards you have promised us through Christ our Lord.

*A Christian's Prayer Book*

***Make Our Lives New***

Spirit, make our lives new by your divine power, that we may live by the light of the resurrection and work in a manner inspired by you. May Christ, our brother, be with us today and every day, now and for ever.

Michael Buckley

***Send Your Peace***

Holy Spirit, I offer myself to your work of healing, peace, and reconciliation. In my busy world bless my silent moments. In the stillness of my heart may I find peace within myself, peace with others, and peace with you.

Michael Buckley

# PRAYING THE SACRAMENTS

The Christian life is nourished by prayer and the sacraments. We celebrate in the sacraments the triumph of Christ over sin, death, and the world. This he achieved through his passion, death, and resurrection. The resurrection of Christ is the ultimate triumph in which the Christian shares through his oneness with the Lord. Since the Resurrection our lives take on a new meaning. No sorrow is ultimate. Christ leads us through everything to final victory. We celebrate all the sacraments because we are an Easter people.

The relationship between God and us is personalized in Christ. God communicates to us through him. Conscious of being "in Christ," the Church sees its sacramental ministry as the continuation of Christ's ministry. As Christ laid his hands on the sick, so does the Church. As he called the Holy Spirit to be his advocate for his followers, so does the Church. As he gave thanks and shared the bread and wine, so the Church represents and calls effectively into the present his sacrifice for our salvation.

The visible signs, or rites, of the sacraments effect and help us to be aware of our personal encounter with Christ. He sanctifies every aspect of our lives, which he presents to our loving Father. Christ meets us in the sacraments at the points of our spiritual growth.

The Christian life, like all life, has a beginning. This is called "initiation." The whole process of initiation marks the beginning of our Christian pilgrimage, which finds its completion in the kingdom of heaven. There, there will be no need of sacraments, because then we will see God face-to-face.

The sacraments of initiation are baptism, confirmation, and Eucharist.

Baptism incorporates us into the body of Christ, the Church, and is the sacrament of new life. Confirmation, which gives us the fullness of the Holy Spirit, is inseparably linked to baptism and is its completion.

The Eucharist, which makes the sacrifice of Christ present and active among us, is the central sacrament in the life of the Church.

There are four other sacraments that help us on our Christian pilgrimage to God, our Father. Reconciliation is the sacrament that restores our relationship with God, whose love we have forsaken through personal sin.

Marriage sanctifies the daily life of husband and wife and their children.

Holy orders perpetuates the special ministry of Christ in his Church.

Anointing of the sick ensures Christ's saving help for us in times of sickness.

From birth to death Christ's resurrection is at work in us. The sacraments are the activity of Christ in our midst, offering praise to the Father and reconciling us to God and to one another.

*Baptism is an Easter sacrament. Through it we are made one with the risen Lord and enter into his risen life.* "All of us who have been baptized into Christ Jesus were baptized into his death…so that as Christ was raised from the dead by the glory of the Father, we too might walk in newness of life" (Romans 6:3–4). *Our "new life" means that we are God's own children in whom Christ's Spirit dwells in a special way. We dare to call God "Abba," Father, for that is what he is to us in this new relationship. We leave spiritual death behind us for the new life of grace.*

## Prayers for Baptism

### *Renewal of Baptismal Vows*

Today I freely acknowledge my commitment to Christ through my baptismal vows, which I renew as a sign and pledge of my Christian faith. I therefore reject Satan and all his works and empty promises. I believe in God, the Father almighty, Creator of heaven and earth. I believe in Jesus Christ, his only Son our Lord, who was born of the Virgin Mary, was crucified, died, and was buried, rose from the dead, and is now seated at the right hand of the Father. I believe in the Holy Spirit, the holy Catholic Church, the communion of saints, the resurrection of the body, and life everlasting. This is my faith. This is the faith of the Church. I am proud to profess it, in Christ Jesus our Lord. Amen.

*Or*

All powerful and merciful God, Father of our Lord Jesus Christ, who freed me from sin and spiritual death and gave me the new life of grace through water and the Holy Spirit, I renew my baptismal vows and rededicate my life to your loving protection, so that day by day, I may grow in your knowledge, love, and service, through Christ our Lord. Amen.

***For the Baptized Person***

Heavenly Father, we pray that this child, true to his (her) baptismal vows, may walk in the light of the resurrection and be true to the gospel of your Son, so that one day he (she) may see you with unveiled face. Amen.

***For the Mother***

God the Father, through his Son, the Virgin Mary's child, has brought joy to all Christian mothers, as they see the hope of eternal life shine on their children. May he bless the mother of this child. She now thanks God for the gift of her child. May she be one with him (her) in thanking God for ever in heaven, in Christ Jesus our Lord. Amen.

***For the Father***

God is the giver of all life, human and divine. May he bless the father of this child. He and his wife will be the first teachers of their child in the ways of faith. May they be also the best of teachers, bearing witness to the faith by what they say and do, in Christ Jesus our Lord. Amen.

### *For Godparents*

Heavenly Father, may the godparents of this child be so inspired by the Holy Spirit that they may always be sensitive to the power of the gospel at work in the life of their godchild. May they lead him (her) by word and example to a true following of Jesus Christ, your only Son our Lord. Amen.

Michael Buckley

### *By Godparents*

Bless us, Lord, that we may fulfill the Christian task entrusted to us. May the example of our lives help our godchild come to a deeper understanding of the Christian faith and so grow in age and wisdom before God and men. Bless our godchild, that he (she) may be faithful to his (her) baptismal vows, and together, as we witness to the gospel, may we all one day behold your sacred countenance. We make this prayer through Christ our Lord. Amen.

Michael Buckley

### *For All Baptized Christians*

By God's gift, through water and the Holy Spirit, we are reborn to everlasting life. In his goodness may he continue to pour out his blessings upon all his sons and daughters. May he make them always, wherever they may be, faithful members of his holy people, and may he send his peace upon all, in Christ Jesus our Lord. Amen.

Michael Buckley

### *For Catechumens*

May their preparation to receive the sacrament of baptism be not merely in their understanding of the teaching of the Church but also in the conduct of their daily lives. Day by day may they be made more ready to be baptized into the body of the risen Lord, share the gifts of the Holy Spirit, and become children of the Father.

### *By Catechumens*

Eternal Father, who created us and made us members of the human family, be with us in our preparation to acknowledge Jesus as Lord of our lives. In all that we say and do, may we be made ready to receive the sacrament that gives us a fuller sharing in gifts of the Holy Spirit and enables us to share at the table of the Lord in the fellowship of his Church.

### *For Better Awareness of Our Baptism*

Lord God, by our baptism into the body of Christ, you have given us a new beginning, a new kind of life. We know that much of our life—our thoughts, feelings, and actions—has not yet been touched or changed by the new life you have given. Help us to see the claims of your love in every part of our life, and having seen them to accept them, so that everything in us may be remade by your love. Through Jesus Christ our Lord.

## Prayers for Confirmation

### *For Those Preparing for Confirmation*

Father, may those who have already been baptized by water and the Holy Spirit persevere faithfully in their Christian vocation. May they fervently receive the sacrament of confirmation, by which they will be given the spirit of wisdom and understanding, the spirit of right judgment and courage, the spirit of knowledge and reverence, and so live the full life of Christians, totally committed to the service of your kingdom.

### *For the Confirmed*

God our Father, complete the work you have begun, and keep the gifts of your Holy Spirit active in the hearts of those who have been confirmed. Make them ready to live his gospel and eager to do his will. May they never be ashamed to proclaim to all the world Christ crucified, living and reigning for ever and ever. Amen.

## THE EUCHARIST: SACRIFICE AND SACRAMENT

*The Eucharist is the center of our relationship with God the Father, Son, and Holy Spirit. It unites us on earth as a community committed to Christ and to one another. As Christians we are, above all else, a Eucharistic community.*

"The Eucharist makes the Church" because it is the center toward which all other sacraments are oriented and the source from which they derive their power. All the sacraments are ideally celebrated within the context of the Eucharist. The Eucharist is, par excellence, the sacred action by which God gives himself to us and through which we give glory to him through our brother and Lord, Jesus the Christ. It is a reciprocal flow, so that God's gift to us in Christ is at the same time our response to him.

The Eucharist is both a sacrifice and a sacrament, since the one essentially involves the other. The victim (sacrifice), Christ, is the meal (sacrament). The Eucharist is a sacrifice that is identified with Calvary. Christ is our paschal lamb who sacrificed himself for us on the cross, so that by his Body and Blood we are nourished as the new people of God.

When we celebrate the Eucharist, we call effectively into our lives the presence of Christ's Body and Blood, soul and divinity, which alone reconciles us to the Father. In it we celebrate, at Christ's command, the memory of what he did for us. We thank him for what he has done, and in joyful anticipation we celebrate the Eucharist until he comes again in glory.

The Eucharist is also a sacrament. St. Paul compares the Church to the body of Christ, of which we are all members. The food for that body is the Eucharist, so Holy Communion makes us a community: The blessing cup that we bless is a communion with the Blood of Christ, and the bread that we break is a communion with the Body of Christ. The fact that there is only one loaf means that, though there are many of us, we form a single body because we all have a share in this one loaf (see 1 Corinthians 10:16–17).

In the Eucharist we share with God and one another in a unique way. The Eucharist is for sanctification and mission. It unites us to God and sends us forth to proclaim to the world the saving power of the Lord Jesus Christ. The Eucharist, the third and final sacrament of initiation, is our pledge of future glory, and we approach the altar remembering the Lord's promise: "He who eats my flesh and drinks my blood has eternal life, and I will raise him up at the last day. For my flesh is food indeed, and my blood is drink indeed. He who eats my flesh and drinks my blood abides in me, and I in him" (John 6:54–56). The Eucharist is a share not only in Christ's death but also in his resurrection.

## THE SACRIFICE OF THE MASS

*The Mass is the effective commemoration of what Christ did for us on the cross. By the power of his Spirit, he re-presents this sacrifice on our altars, so that honor, praise, adoration, and thanksgiving may be continually given to the Father. The Mass is filled with joy and hope, because in it we celebrate the Lord's death and resurrection until he comes again. In one action it telescopes all time, past, present, and future.*

### Prayers Before Mass

#### *To the Holy Trinity*

Receive, most Holy Trinity, this holy sacrifice of the Body and Blood of our Lord Jesus Christ, which by the hands of your priest, I, your unworthy servant, now offer to your divine majesty. I unite it with all the Masses that have ever been or will be offered to you, in union with the sacrifice of Christ our Lord on the cross, and according to his will and that of his holy Church. Through it may I share in the resurrection of your Son, who in rising from the dead is our sure hope of eternal salvation.

#### *For the Sanctification of Sunday*

Almighty and eternal God, who has appointed six days in which we may labor and has consecrated the seventh to yourself, grant that we may sanctify this day as you have commanded by devoting it to your service. Mercifully forgive us all our past neglect, pardon the sins of which we have been guilty during the week, and give us the grace to avoid them for the future.

***An Offering Prayer***

Most merciful Father, you so loved the world that you sent your only Son to redeem and save us. In obedience to your will, he humbled himself, even to death on a cross. He continues to offer himself daily through the ministry of his priests for the living and the dead. We humbly pray that, motivated by a living faith, we may always assist with devotion and reverence at the oblation of his most precious Body and Blood that is made at Mass. In this way we share in the supreme sacrifice that he accomplished on Calvary and in his resurrection from the dead.

In union with the whole Church, and in the company of the Blessed Virgin Mary and all the angels and saints, we now offer the adorable sacrifice of the Mass to your honor and glory. In it we acknowledge your infinite perfections, your supreme dominion over all creatures, our entire submission to you, and our dependence on your gracious providence. We offer it in thanksgiving for your goodness to us and for the forgiveness of our sins.

We offer it also for the spread of the Catholic Church throughout the world and for our pope, bishop, and all the pastors, that they may direct the faithful in the way of salvation. In this Mass we pray for peace and goodwill among all peoples and for the needs of our world. May we here present receive grace to live a Christian life in this world in order to be with you in the world to come. We offer this Mass for the eternal repose of the faithful departed.

In this Mass we remember with gratitude all that your Son Jesus Christ suffered for love of us, as we commemorate his bitter passion and death, his glorious resurrection and ascension into heaven. We offer it for all the intentions agreeable to your holy will, through the same Jesus Christ, your Son, our Lord, who is both priest and victim. We make our prayer in the name of the most Holy Trinity—Father, Son, and Holy Spirit—to whom be honor, praise, and glory for ever and ever. Amen.

### *To God the Father*

Eternal Father, I offer you all the Masses celebrated this day throughout the world for sinners in their agony and for those who shall be overtaken by death today. May they obtain mercy through the precious blood of Jesus their redeemer, and may the same precious blood obtain satisfaction for my sins and a share in the resurrection of your Son. Amen.

### *To God the Son*

Lord Jesus Christ, to whom belongs all that is in heaven and earth, I desire to consecrate myself wholly to you and to be yours for evermore. This day I offer myself to you in singleness of heart, to serve and obey you always, and I offer you without ceasing a sacrifice of praise and thanksgiving. Receive me, O my Savior, in union with the holy oblation of your precious blood that I offer to you this day, in the presence of angels, that this sacrifice may avail unto my salvation and that of the whole world.

Thomas à Kempis

### *At the Lamb's High Feast*

At the Lamb's high feast we sing
praise to our victorious king,
who hath washed us in the tide
flowing from his pierced side.
Praise we him whose love divine
gives the guests his blood for wine,
gives his body for the feast,
love the victim, love the priest.

Where the paschal blood is poured,
Death's dark angel sheathes his sword;
Israel's hosts triumphant go
through the wave that drowns the foe.
Christ the Lamb, whose blood was shed,
Paschal victim, paschal bread,
with sincerity and love
eat we manna from above.

Mighty victim from the sky,
powers of hell beneath thee lie;
death is conquered in the fight;
thou hast brought us life and light.
Now thy banner thou dost wave;
vanquished Satan and the grave;
angels join his praise to tell—
see o'erthrown the prince of hell.

Paschal triumph, paschal joy,
only sin can this destroy;

from the death of sin set free
souls reborn, dear Lord, in thee.
Hymns of glory, songs of praise,
Father, unto thee we raise.
Risen Lord, all praise to thee,
ever with the Spirit be.

Seventh century, translation by Robert Campbell

***To God the Holy Spirit***

Holy Spirit, cleanse our minds and hearts so that we may celebrate with joy the mysteries of our redemption in this holy Mass. Be near us as we bring our gifts to the Father, in union with the Son, who as our supreme high priest has gone through to the highest heaven, there to make intercession for us. Fill us with confidence in approaching the throne of grace, where with all the angels and saints, we shall render due homage through Jesus Christ, who with you and the Father lives and reigns, God, for ever and ever. Amen.

***To Our Lady***

Mother of mercy and love, blessed Virgin Mary, I turn to you in confidence. You stood by your Son as he hung dying on the cross. Stand also by me and by all those who assist at Mass today, here and throughout the entire Church. Help us to offer a perfect and acceptable sacrifice in the sight of the holy and undivided Trinity, our most high God.

***To St. Joseph***

God, our Father, just as you allowed Joseph to touch with his hands and bear in his arms your only Son, Jesus Christ, so also may we, through cleanness of heart and blamelessness of life, be worthy to assist at Mass, and thus may we be better prepared for the banquet of the kingdom.

***To Our Guardian Angel and All the Saints***

May my guardian angel and all the saints, especially my patron St. N., intercede for me, that I may be worthy to assist in offering this sacrifice to almighty God, for the praise and glory of his name, for our good and the good of all his Church.

***To the Saint of the Day***

St. N., in whose honor the holy sacrifice of the Body and Blood is this day offered to God the Father, intercede for me with the Holy Spirit, that I be given the grace to participate in this great sacrifice in a worthy and acceptable manner, and so with you and all the saints come to sing the praises of God eternally in our heavenly home.

***Excerpts From the Psalms***

I was glad when they said to me,
  "Let us go to the house of the LORD!"
Our feet have been standing
  within your gates, O Jerusalem!
. . .
For my brethren and companions' sake
  I will say, "Peace be within you!"
For the sake of the house of the LORD our God,
  I will seek your good.

Psalm 122:1–2, 8–9

Make a joyful noise to the LORD, all the lands.
Serve the LORD with gladness!
Come into his presence with singing!
...
Enter his gates with thanksgiving,
  and his courts with praise!
  Give thanks to him, bless his name!

Psalm 100:1–2, 4

How lovely is your dwelling place,
  O LORD of hosts!
My soul longs, yes, faints
  for the courts of the LORD;
...
Blessed are those who dwell in your house,
  ever singing your praise!
...
For a day in your courts is better
  than a thousand elsewhere.

Psalm 84:1–2, 4, 10

## The Order of Mass

### INTRODUCTORY RITES

***Entrance Procession***

*All stand for the entrance song or antiphon of the day.*

In the name of the Father, and of the Son, and of the Holy Spirit.
Amen.

***Greeting***
*The priest greets the people in one of the following ways:*

1. The grace of our Lord Jesus Christ, and the love of God, and the communion of the Holy Spirit be with you all.
*Or*
2. Grace to you and peace from God our Father and the Lord Jesus Christ.
*Or*
3. The Lord be with you.
*Or, if a bishop presides:*
4. Peace be with you.

*The people reply:*
**And with your spirit.**

***Theme of the Mass***
*The priest, or a deacon, or another minister may briefly introduce the theme of the day's Mass.*

***Penitential Act***
*The priest invites the faithful to recall their sins:*

Brethren (brothers and sisters), let us acknowledge our sins, and so prepare ourselves to celebrate the sacred mysteries.
*After a brief silence one of the following forms is used:*

**1. I confess to almighty God**
**and to you, my brothers and sisters,**
**that I have greatly sinned,**
**in my thoughts and in my words,**
**in what I have done and in what I have failed to do,**

*All strike their breast as they say:*

**through my fault, through my fault,**
**through my most grievous fault;**

**therefore I ask blessed Mary ever-Virgin,**
**all the angels and saints,**
**and you, my brothers and sisters,**
**to pray for me to the Lord our God.**

**2. Have mercy on us, O Lord.**
**For we have sinned against you.**
**Show us, O Lord, your mercy.**
**And grant us your salvation.**

3. *The priest, a deacon, or another minister says the following or similar invocations*:
You were sent to heal the contrite of heart: Lord, have mercy.
*Or*
Kyrie, eleison.

**Lord, have mercy.**

*Or*

**Kyrie, eleison.**

You came to call sinners: Christ, have mercy.
*Or*
Christe, eleison.

**Christ, have mercy.**

*Or*

**Christe, eleison.**

You are seated at the right hand of the Father to intercede for us: Lord, have mercy.

*Or*

Kyrie, eleison.

**Lord, have mercy.**

*Or*

**Kyrie, eleison.**

*The absolution by the priest follows:*

May almighty God have mercy on us,
forgive us our sins,
and bring us to everlasting life.

**Amen.**

*If form 1 of the Penitential Act was used, the following invocations are then said or sung:*

Lord, have mercy.

**Lord, have mercy.**

Christ, have mercy.

**Christ, have mercy.**

Lord, have mercy.

**Lord, have mercy.**

*Or*

Kyrie, eleison.

**Kyrie, eleison.**

Christe, eleison.

**Christe, eleison.**

Kyrie, eleison.

**Kyrie, eleison.**

***Rite of Sprinkling***

*From time to time on Sundays, especially in Easter Time, instead of the customary Penitential Act, the blessing and sprinkling of water may take place as a reminder of baptism. One of the following is prayed:*

1. Dear brethren (brothers and sisters),
let us humbly beseech the Lord our God
to bless this water he has created,
which will be sprinkled on us
as a memorial of our baptism.
May he help us by his grace
to remain faithful to the Spirit we have received.

*After a brief silence the priest joins his hands and prays:*
Almighty ever-living God,
who willed that through water,
the fountain of life and the source of purification,
even souls should be cleansed
and receive the gift of eternal life;
be pleased, we pray, to bless + this water,
by which we seek protection on this your day, O Lord.
Renew the living spring of your grace within us
and grant that by this water we may be defended
from all ills of spirit and body,
and so approach you with hearts made clean
and worthily receive your salvation.
Through Christ our Lord.

**Amen.**

2. Almighty Lord and God,
who are the source and origin of all life,
whether of body or soul,
we ask you to + bless this water,
which we use in confidence
to implore forgiveness for our sins
and to obtain the protection of your grace
against all illness and every snare of the enemy.
Grant, O Lord, in your mercy,
that living waters may always spring up for our salvation,
and so may we approach you with a pure heart
and avoid all danger to body and soul.
Through Christ our Lord.

**Amen.**

3. *During the Easter season*
Lord our God,
in your mercy be present to your people's prayers,
and for us who recall the wondrous work of our creation
and the still greater work of our redemption,
graciously + bless this water.
For you created water to make the fields fruitful
and to refresh and cleanse our bodies.
You also made water the instrument of your mercy:
for through water you freed your people from slavery
and quenched their thirst in the desert;
through water the prophets proclaimed the new covenant
you were to enter upon with the human race;
and last of all,

through water, which Christ made holy in the Jordan,
you have renewed our corrupted nature
in the bath of regeneration.
Therefore, may this water be for us
a memorial of the baptism we have received,
and grant that we may share
in the gladness of our brothers and sisters
who at Easter have received their baptism.
Through Christ our Lord.

**Amen.**

*Where the circumstances of the place or the custom of the people suggest, the priest may bless salt:*

We humbly ask you, almighty God:
be pleased in your faithful love to + bless this salt
you have created,
for it was you who commanded the prophet Elisha
to cast salt into water,
that impure water might be purified.
Grant, O Lord, we pray,
that, wherever this mixture of salt and water is sprinkled,
every attack of the enemy may be repulsed
and your Holy Spirit may be present
to keep us safe at all times.
Through Christ our Lord.

**Amen.**

*The priest pours the salt into the water.*
*The priest sprinkles himself and the minsters, then the clergy and the people. An appropriate chant is sung. The rite concludes with this prayer:*
May almighty God cleanse us of our sins
and, through the celebration of this Eucharist,
make us worthy to share at the table of his kingdom.
**Amen.**

***Gloria***

*This triumphant hymn of praise is sung or said by all on Sundays outside of Advent and Lent, on solemnities and feasts, and on some other occasions of special importance.*

**Glory to God in the highest,**
**and on earth peace to people of good will.**
**We praise you, we bless you,**
**we adore you, we glorify you,**
**we give you thanks for your great glory,**
**Lord God, heavenly King,**
**O God, almighty Father.**

**Lord Jesus Christ, only begotten Son,**
**Lord God, Lamb of God, Son of the Father,**
**you take away the sins of the world,**
**have mercy on us;**
**you take away the sins of the world,**
**receive our prayer;**
**you are seated at the right hand of the Father,**
**have mercy on us.**

**For you alone are the Holy One,**
**you alone are the Lord,**
**you alone are the Most High,**
**Jesus Christ,**
**with the Holy Spirit,**
**in the glory of God the Father.**
**Amen.**

***Opening Prayer***

Let us pray.

*All pray in silence. Then the priest, with hands extended, says the Opening Prayer for the day, at the end of which the people acclaim:* Amen.

THE LITURGY OF THE WORD

***First Reading***

*All sit.*

*At the end of the reading, the reader acclaims:*

The word of the Lord.

**Thanks be to God.**

***Responsorial Psalm***

*The cantor or reader sings or recites the psalm, with the people making the response.*

***Second Reading*** (on Sundays and other feasts)

*To indicate the end of the reading, the reader acclaims:*

The word of the Lord.

**Thanks be to God.**

***Proclamation of the Gospel***

*All stand for the Alleluia or another chant laid down by the rubrics, as the liturgical time requires. Meanwhile, if incense is used, the priest puts some into the thurible. The deacon who is to proclaim the Gospel, bowing profoundly before the priest, asks for the blessing in a low voice:*

Your blessing, Father.

*The priest says in a low voice:*

May the Lord be in your heart and on your lips,
that you may proclaim his Gospel worthily and well,
in the name of the Father and of the Son and of the Holy Spirit.

*The deacon signs himself with the Sign of the Cross and replies:*

Amen.

*If a deacon is not present, the priest, bowing before the altar, says quietly:*

Cleanse my heart and my lips, almighty God,
that I may worthily proclaim your holy Gospel.

*The deacon or priest goes to the ambo and addresses the congregation:*

The Lord be with you.

**And with your spirit.**

A reading from the holy Gospel according to N.

*He makes the Sign of the Cross on the book and on his forehead, lips, and breast.*

**Glory to you, O Lord.**

*At the end of the Gospel, the deacon or priest acclaims:*
The Gospel of the Lord.

**Praise to you, Lord Jesus Christ.**

***Homily***
*All sit.*

***Profession of Faith***
*All stand.*

**I believe in one God,**
**the Father almighty,**
**maker of heaven and earth,**
**of all things visible and invisible.**

**I believe in one Lord Jesus Christ,**
**the only begotten Son of God,**
**born of the Father before all ages.**
**God from God, Light from Light,**
**true God from true God,**
**begotten, not made, consubstantial with the Father;**
**through him all things were made.**
**For us men and for our salvation**
**he came down from heaven,**

*Up to and including "and became man," all bow.*

**and by the Holy Spirit was incarnate of the Virgin Mary,**
**and became man.**

**For our sake he was crucified under Pontius Pilate,**
**he suffered death and was buried,**

**and rose again on the third day**
**in accordance with the Scriptures.**
**He ascended into heaven**
**and is seated at the right hand of the Father.**
**He will come again in glory**
**to judge the living and the dead,**
**and his kingdom will have no end.**

**I believe in the Holy Spirit, the Lord, the giver of life,**
**who proceeds from the Father and the Son,**
**who with the Father and the Son is adored and glorified,**
**who has spoken through the prophets.**

**I believe in one, holy, catholic, and apostolic Church.**
**I confess one baptism for the forgiveness of sins,**
**and I look forward to the resurrection of the dead**
**and the life of the world to come.**
**Amen.**

*The Apostles' Creed, which is the baptismal symbol of the Roman Church, may be used instead of the Niceno-Constantinopolitan Creed, especially during Lent and Easter Time:*

**I believe in God,**
**the Father almighty,**
**Creator of heaven and earth,**
**and in Jesus Christ, his only Son, our Lord,**

*At the words that follow, up to and including "the Virgin Mary," all bow.*

**who was conceived by the Holy Spirit,**
**born of the Virgin Mary,**
**suffered under Pontius Pilate,**
**was crucified, died, and was buried;**
**he descended into hell;**
**on the third day he rose again from the dead;**

**he ascended into heaven**
**and is seated at the right hand of God the Father almighty;**
**from there he will come to judge the living and the dead.**
**I believe in the Holy Spirit,**
**the holy catholic Church,**
**the communion of saints,**
**the forgiveness of sins,**
**the resurrection of the body,**
**and life everlasting. Amen.**

***Prayer of the Faithful***

*The people respond to each intercession with*

**Lord, hear our prayer**

*or a similar response. The priest says a concluding prayer, to which the people respond:*

**Amen.**

THE LITURGY OF THE EUCHARIST

***Presentation and Preparation of the Gifts***

*A hymn may be sung. Otherwise the people make their responses to the prayers of offering:*

Blessed are you, Lord God of all creation,
for through your goodness we have received
the bread we offer you:
Fruit of the earth and work of human hands,
it will become for us the bread of life.

**Blessed be God for ever.**

By the mystery of this water and wine,
may we come to share in the divinity of Christ,
who humbled himself to share in our humanity.

Blessed are you, Lord God of all creation,
for through your goodness we have received
the wine we offer you:
Fruit of the vine and work of human hands,
it will become our spiritual drink.

**Blessed be God for ever.**

With humble spirit and contrite heart,
may we be accepted by you, O Lord,
and may our sacrifice in your sight this day
be pleasing to you, Lord God.

*The priest may incense the offerings, the cross, and the altar. A deacon or other minister then incenses the priest and the people. Then the priest, standing at the side of the altar, washes his hands, saying quietly:*

Wash me, O Lord, from my iniquity
and cleanse me from my sin.

***Prayer Over the Gifts***

Pray, brethren (brothers and sisters), that my sacrifice and yours may be acceptable to God, the almighty Father.

*The people rise and reply:*

**May the Lord accept the sacrifice at your hands**
**for the praise and glory of his name,**
**for our good and the good of all his holy Church.**

*The priest prays from the Proper of the Day, at the end of which the people acclaim:*

**Amen.**

***The Eucharistic Prayer***

PREFACE

The Lord be with you.

**And with your spirit.**

Lift up your hearts.

**We lift them up to the Lord.**

Let us give thanks to the Lord our God.

**It is right and just.**

*The priest prays one of the many Prefaces, in accord with the rubrics. (Eucharistic Prayers II and IV have their own Prefaces; see pages 108 and 116). At the end of the Preface, all sing or say aloud:*

**Holy, Holy, Holy Lord God of hosts.**
**Heaven and earth are full of your glory.**
**Hosanna in the highest.**
**Blessed is he who comes in the name of the Lord.**

**Hosanna in the highest.**

*All kneel.*

There are many ways of thanking God for all he has accomplished for us through Christ.

Eucharistic Prayer I, see page 102.
Eucharistic Prayer II, see page 108.
Eucharistic Prayer III, see page 112.
Eucharistic Prayer IV, see page 116.

***Eucharistic Prayer I (The Roman Canon)***

*The words in brackets may be omitted.*

To you, therefore, most merciful Father,
we make humble prayer and petition
through Jesus Christ, your Son, our Lord:
that you accept
and bless these gifts, these offerings,
these holy and unblemished sacrifices,
which we offer you firstly
for your holy catholic Church.
*We pray for the Church.*
Be pleased to grant her peace,
to guard, unite, and govern her
throughout the whole world,
together with your servant N. our pope
and N. our bishop,
and all those who, holding to the truth,
hand on the catholic and apostolic faith.
*We pray for the living.*

Remember, Lord, your servants N. and N.
*(The priest prays briefly for those mentioned.)*
and all gathered here,
whose faith and devotion are known to you.
For them we offer you this sacrifice of praise
or they offer it for themselves
and all who are dear to them:
for the redemption of their souls,
in hope of health and well-being,
and paying their homage to you,
the eternal God, living and true.
*In communion with the saints*
In communion with those whose memory we venerate,
especially the glorious ever-Virgin Mary,
Mother of our God and Lord, Jesus Christ,
+ and blessed Joseph, her spouse,
your blessed apostles and martyrs,
Peter and Paul, Andrew,
[James, John, Thomas, James, Philip,
Bartholomew, Matthew, Simon and Jude;
Linus, Cletus, Clement, Sixtus, Cornelius, Cyprian,
Lawrence, Chrysogonus, John and Paul, Cosmas and Damian]
and all your saints;
we ask that through their merits and prayers,
in all things we may be defended by your protecting help.
[Through Christ our Lord. Amen.]
*Special prayers are added here to mark the feasts of Christmas, Epiphany, Easter, the Ascension, and Pentecost.*

*Holding his hands extended over the offerings, the priest says:*
Be pleased, O God, we pray,
to bless, acknowledge,
and approve this offering in every respect;
make it spiritual and acceptable,
so that it may become for us
the Body and Blood of your most beloved Son,
our Lord Jesus Christ.

*The Lord's Supper: The Consecration*
On the day before he was to suffer,
he took bread in his holy and venerable hands,
and with eyes raised to heaven,
to you, O God, his almighty Father,
giving you thanks, he said the blessing,
broke the bread,
and gave it to his disciples, saying:
TAKE THIS, ALL OF YOU, AND EAT OF IT,
FOR THIS IS MY BODY,
WHICH WILL BE GIVEN UP FOR YOU.

In a similar way, when supper was ended,
he took this precious chalice
in his holy and venerable hands,
and once more giving you thanks, he said the blessing
and gave the chalice to his disciples, saying:
TAKE THIS, ALL OF YOU, AND DRINK FROM IT,
FOR THIS IS THE CHALICE OF MY BLOOD,
THE BLOOD OF THE NEW AND ETERNAL COVENANT,

WHICH WILL BE POURED OUT FOR YOU AND FOR MANY
FOR THE FORGIVENESS OF SINS.
DO THIS IN MEMORY OF ME.

The mystery of faith.

**1. We proclaim your death, O Lord,**
**and profess your resurrection**
**until you come again.**

*Or*

**2. When we eat this Bread and drink this cup,**
**we proclaim your death, O Lord,**
**until you come again.**

*Or*

**3. Save us, Savior of the world,**
**for by your cross and resurrection**
**you have set us free.**

Therefore, O Lord,
as we celebrate the memorial of the blessed passion,
the resurrection from the dead,
and the glorious ascension into heaven
of Christ, your Son, our Lord,
we, your servants and your holy people,
offer to your glorious majesty from the gifts that you have given us,
this pure victim, this holy victim, this spotless victim,
the holy Bread of eternal life and the chalice of everlasting salvation.

Be pleased to look upon these offerings
with a serene and kindly countenance,
and to accept them,
as once you were pleased to accept
the gifts of your servant Abel the just,
the sacrifice of Abraham, our father in faith,
and the offering of your high priest Melchizedek,
a holy sacrifice, a spotless victim.

In humble prayer we ask you, almighty God:
command that these gifts be borne
by the hands of your holy angel
to your altar on high
in the sight of your divine majesty,
so that all of us, who through this participation at the altar
receive the most holy Body and Blood of your Son,
may be filled with every grace and heavenly blessing.
[Through Christ our Lord. Amen.]

*For the dead*
Remember also, Lord, your servants N. and N.,
who have gone before us with the sign of faith
and rest in the sleep of peace.

*The priest joins his hands and prays briefly.*
Grant them, O Lord, we pray,
and all who sleep in Christ,
a place of refreshment, light, and peace.
[Through Christ our Lord. Amen.]

*The priest strikes his breast with his right hand, saying:*
To us also, your servants, who though sinners
hope in your abundant mercies,
graciously grant some share
and fellowship with your holy apostles and martyrs:
with John the Baptist, Stephen, Matthias, Barnabas,
[Ignatius, Alexander, Marcellinus, Peter,
Felicity, Perpetua, Agatha, Lucy,
Agnes, Cecilia, Anastasia]
and all your saints;
admit us, we beseech you,
into their company,
not weighing our merits but granting us your pardon,
through Christ our Lord.

Through whom you continue to make all these good things,
O Lord;
you sanctify them, fill them with life,
bless them, and bestow them upon us.

*Final Doxology*
Through him, and with him, and in him,
O God, almighty Father,
in the unity of the Holy Spirit,
all glory and honor is yours,
for ever and ever.
**Amen.**

*The Communion Rite follows, page 122.*

### *Eucharistic Prayer II*

*Although it is provided with its own Preface, this Eucharistic Prayer may also be used with other Prefaces, especially those that present an overall view of the mystery of salvation.*

PREFACE

It is truly right and just, our duty and our salvation,
always and everywhere to give you thanks,
Father most holy,
through your beloved Son, Jesus Christ,
your Word through whom you made all things,
whom you sent as our Savior and Redeemer,
incarnate by the Holy Spirit and born of the Virgin.

Fulfilling your will and gaining for you a holy people,
he stretched out his hands as he endured his passion,
so as to break the bonds of death and manifest the resurrection.
And so, with the angels and all the saints
we declare your glory,
as with one voice we acclaim:

> **Holy, Holy, Holy Lord God of hosts.**
> **Heaven and earth are full of your glory.**
> **Hosanna in the highest.**
> **Blessed is he who comes in the name of the Lord.**
> **Hosanna in the highest.**

*All kneel.*

You are indeed holy, O Lord,
the fount of all holiness.

Make holy, therefore, these gifts, we pray,
by sending down your Spirit upon them like the dewfall,
so that they may become for us
the Body and Blood of our Lord Jesus Christ.

*The Lord's Supper*
At the time he was betrayed
and entered willingly into his passion,
he took bread and, giving thanks, broke it,
and gave it to his disciples, saying:
TAKE THIS, ALL OF YOU, AND EAT OF IT,
FOR THIS IS MY BODY,
WHICH WILL BE GIVEN UP FOR YOU.

In a similar way, when supper was ended,
he took the chalice
and, once more giving thanks,
he gave it to his disciples, saying:
TAKE THIS, ALL OF YOU, AND DRINK FROM IT,
FOR THIS IS THE CHALICE OF MY BLOOD,
THE BLOOD OF THE NEW AND ETERNAL COVENANT,
WHICH WILL BE POURED OUT FOR YOU AND FOR MANY
FOR THE FORGIVENESS OF SINS.
DO THIS IN MEMORY OF ME.

The mystery of faith.

**1. We proclaim your death, O Lord,
and profess your resurrection
until you come again.**

*Or*

**2. When we eat this Bread and drink this cup,**
**we proclaim your death, O Lord,**
**until you come again.**

*Or*

**3. Save us, Savior of the world,**
**for by your cross and resurrection**
**you have set us free.**

Therefore, as we celebrate
the memorial of his death and resurrection,
we offer you, Lord,
the Bread of life and the chalice of salvation,
giving thanks that you have held us worthy
to be in your presence and minister to you.

Humbly we pray that,
partaking of the Body and Blood of Christ,
we may be gathered into one by the Holy Spirit.

*Intercessions for the Church*
Remember, Lord, your Church,
spread throughout the world,
and bring her to the fullness of charity,
together with N. our pope and N. our bishop
and all the clergy.

*In Masses for the Dead, the following may be added:*
Remember your servant N.,
whom you have called [today]
from this world to yourself.

Grant that he (she), who was united with your Son in a death like his,
may also be one with him in his resurrection.

*For All the Dead*
Remember also our brothers and sisters
who have fallen asleep in the hope of the resurrection,
and all who have died in your mercy:
welcome them into the light of your face.

*In Communion With the Saints*
Have mercy on us all, we pray,
that with the Blessed Virgin Mary, Mother of God,
with the blessed apostles,
and all the saints who have pleased you throughout the ages,
we may merit to be coheirs to eternal life,
and may praise and glorify you
through your Son, Jesus Christ.

*Final Doxology*
Through him, and with him, and in him,
O God, almighty Father,
in the unity of the Holy Spirit,
all glory and honor is yours,
for ever and ever.
**Amen.**

*The Communion Rite follows, page 122.*

***Eucharistic Prayer III***

*Praise to the Father*

You are indeed holy, O Lord,
and all you have created rightly gives you praise,
for through your Son our Lord Jesus Christ,
by the power and working of the Holy Spirit,
you give life to all things and make them holy,
and you never cease to gather a people to yourself,
so that from the rising of the sun to its setting
a pure sacrifice may be offered to your name.

*Invocation of the Holy Spirit*

Therefore, O Lord, we humbly implore you:
by the same Spirit graciously make holy
these gifts we have brought to you for consecration,
that they may become the Body and Blood
of your Son our Lord Jesus Christ,
at whose command we celebrate these mysteries.

*The Lord's Supper: The Consecration*

For on the night he was betrayed
he himself took bread,
and giving you thanks, he said the blessing,
broke the bread, and gave it to his disciples, saying:
TAKE THIS, ALL OF YOU, AND EAT OF IT,
FOR THIS IS MY BODY,
WHICH WILL BE GIVEN UP FOR YOU.

In a similar way, when supper was ended,
he took the chalice,

and giving you thanks, he said the blessing
and gave the chalice to his disciples, saying:
TAKE THIS, ALL OF YOU, AND DRINK FROM IT,
FOR THIS IS THE CHALICE OF MY BLOOD,
THE BLOOD OF THE NEW AND ETERNAL COVENANT,
WHICH WILL BE POURED OUT FOR YOU AND FOR MANY
FOR THE FORGIVENESS OF SINS.
DO THIS IN MEMORY OF ME.

The mystery of faith.

**1. We proclaim your death, O Lord,
and profess your resurrection
until you come again.**

*Or*

**2. When we eat this Bread and drink this cup,
we proclaim your death, O Lord,
until you come again.**

*Or*

**3. Save us, Savior of the world,
for by your cross and resurrection
you have set us free.**

Therefore, O Lord, as we celebrate the memorial
of the saving passion of your Son,
his wondrous resurrection and ascension into heaven,
and as we look forward to his second coming,
we offer you in thanksgiving this holy and living sacrifice.

Look, we pray, upon the oblation of your Church,
and recognizing the sacrificial Victim by whose death you

willed
to reconcile us to yourself,
grant that we who are nourished by the Body and Blood of your Son
and filled with his Holy Spirit
may become one body, one spirit in Christ.

*In Communion With the Saints*
May he make of us an eternal offering to you,
so that we may obtain an inheritance with your elect,
especially with the most Blessed Virgin Mary, Mother of God,
with your blessed apostles and glorious martyrs,
[with Saint N.: the saint of the day or patron saint]
and with all the saints,
on whose constant intercession in your presence
we rely for unfailing help.

*Intercessions for the Church*
May this Sacrifice of our reconciliation,
we pray, O Lord,
advance the peace and salvation of all the world.
Be pleased to confirm in faith and charity
your pilgrim Church on earth,
with your servant N. our pope and N. our bishop,
the order of bishops, all the clergy,
and the entire people you have gained for your own.

Listen graciously to the prayers of this family,
whom you have summoned before you:
In your compassion, O merciful Father,

gather to yourself all your children
scattered throughout the world.

*For the Dead and for the Living*
To our departed brothers and sisters
and to all who were pleasing to you
at their passing from this life,
give kind admittance to your kingdom.
There we hope to enjoy for ever the fullness of your glory
through Christ our Lord,
through whom you bestow on the world all that is good.

*In Masses for the Dead, the following may be said instead of the above:*
Remember your servant N.
whom you have called [today] from this world to yourself.
Grant that he (she), who was united with your Son in a death like his,
may also be one with him in his resurrection,
when from the earth he will raise up in the flesh those who have died
and transform our lowly body after the pattern of his own glorious body.
To our departed brothers and sisters too,
and to all who were pleasing to you at their passing from this life,
give kind admittance to your kingdom.
There we hope to enjoy for ever the fullness of your glory,
when you will wipe away every tear from our eyes.

For seeing you, our God, as you are,
we shall be like you for all the ages and praise you without end,
through Christ our Lord,
through whom you bestow on the world all that is good. +

*Final Doxology*
Through him, and with him, and in him,
O God, almighty Father,
in the unity of the Holy Spirit,
all glory and honor is yours, for ever and ever.
**Amen.**

*The Communion Rite follows, page 122.*

***Eucharistic Prayer IV***
*The following Preface must be prayed to conform with the structure of Eucharistic Prayer IV:*
It is truly right to give you thanks,
truly just to give you glory, Father most holy,
for you are the one God living and true,
existing before all ages and abiding for all eternity,
dwelling in unapproachable light;
yet you, who alone are good, the source of life,
have made all that is,
so that you might fill your creatures with blessings
and bring joy to many of them by the glory of your light.

And so in your presence are countless hosts of angels,
who serve you day and night

and, gazing upon the glory of your face,
glorify you without ceasing.
With them we too confess your name in exultation,
giving voice to every creature under heaven,
as we acclaim:

**Holy, Holy, Holy Lord God of hosts.**
**Heaven and earth are full of your glory.**
**Hosanna in the highest.**
**Blessed is he who comes in the name of the Lord.**
**Hosanna in the highest.**

*Praise to the Father*
We give you praise, Father most holy,
for you are great,
and you have fashioned all your works
in wisdom and in love.
You formed man in your own image
and entrusted the whole world to his care,
so that in serving you alone, the Creator, he might have dominion over all creatures.
And when through disobedience he had lost your friendship,
you did not abandon him to the domain of death.
For you came in mercy to the aid of all,
so that those who seek might find you.
Time and again you offered them covenants
and through the prophets
taught them to look forward to salvation.

And you so loved the world, Father most holy,
that in the fullness of time
you sent your only begotten Son to be our Savior.
Made incarnate by the Holy Spirit
and born of the Virgin Mary,
he shared our human nature
in all things but sin.
To the poor he proclaimed the good news of salvation,
to prisoners, freedom,
and to the sorrowful of heart, joy.
To accomplish your plan,
he gave himself up to death,
and rising from the dead,
he destroyed death and restored life.

And that we might live no longer for ourselves
but for him who died and rose again for us,
he sent the Holy Spirit from you, Father,
as the first fruits for those who believe,
so that, bringing to perfection his work in the world,
he might sanctify creation to the full.

*Invocation of the Holy Spirit*
Therefore, O Lord, we pray:
may this same Holy Spirit
graciously sanctify these offerings,
that they may become
the Body and Blood of our Lord Jesus Christ
for the celebration of this great mystery,

which he himself left us
as an eternal covenant.

*The Lord's Supper: The Consecration*
For when the hour had come
for him to be glorified by you, Father most holy,
having loved his own who were in the world,
he loved them to the end:
and while they were at supper,
he took bread, blessed and broke it,
and gave it to his disciples, saying,
TAKE THIS, ALL OF YOU, AND EAT OF IT,
FOR THIS IS MY BODY,
WHICH WILL BE GIVEN UP FOR YOU.

In a similar way,
taking the chalice filled with the fruit of the vine,
he gave thanks
and gave the chalice to his disciples, saying:
TAKE THIS, ALL OF YOU, AND DRINK FROM IT,
FOR THIS IS THE CHALICE OF MY BLOOD,
THE BLOOD OF THE NEW AND ETERNAL COVENANT,
WHICH WILL BE POURED OUT FOR YOU AND FOR MANY
FOR THE FORGIVENESS OF SINS.
DO THIS IN MEMORY OF ME.
The mystery of faith.

**1. We proclaim your death, O Lord,
and profess your resurrection
until you come again.**

*Or*

**2. When we eat this Bread and drink this cup,
we proclaim your death, O Lord,
until you come again.**

*Or*

**3. Save us, Savior of the world,
for by your cross and resurrection
you have set us free.**

Therefore, O Lord,
as we now celebrate the memorial of our redemption,
we remember Christ's death
and his descent to the realm of the dead,
we proclaim his resurrection
and his ascension to your right hand,
and as we await his coming in glory,
we offer you his Body and Blood,
the sacrifice acceptable to you
which brings salvation to the whole world.

Look, O Lord, upon the Sacrifice
which you yourself have provided for your Church,
and grant in your loving kindness
to all who partake of this one Bread and one chalice
that, gathered into one body by the Holy Spirit,
they may truly become a living sacrifice in Christ
to the praise of your glory.

*Intercessions for the Church*

Therefore, Lord, remember now
all for whom we offer this sacrifice:
especially your servant N. our pope,
N. our bishop, and the whole order of bishops,
all the clergy, those who take part in this offering,
those gathered here before you, your entire people,
and all who seek you with a sincere heart.

*For the Dead*

Remember also those who have died in the peace of your Christ
and all the dead,
whose faith you alone have known.

*In Communion With the Saints*

To all of us, your children,
grant, O merciful Father,
that we may enter into a heavenly inheritance
with the Blessed Virgin Mary, Mother of God,
and with your apostles and saints in your kingdom.
There, with the whole of creation,
freed from the corruption of sin and death,
may we glorify you through Christ our Lord,
through whom you bestow on the world all that is good.

*Final Doxology*

Through him, and with him, and in him,
O God, almighty Father,
in the unity of the Holy Spirit,

all glory and honor is yours, for ever and ever.

**Amen.**

THE COMMUNION RITE

*All stand.*

***The Lord's Prayer***

At the Savior's command
and formed by divine teaching,
we dare to say:

**Our Father, who art in heaven,**
**hallowed be thy name;**
**thy kingdom come,**
**thy will be done**
**on earth as it is in heaven.**
**Give us this day our daily bread,**
**and forgive us our trespasses,**
**as we forgive those who trespass against us;**
**and lead us not into temptation,**
**but deliver us from evil.**

Deliver us, Lord, we pray, from every evil,
graciously grant peace in our days,
that by the help of your mercy,
we may be always free from sin
and safe from all distress,
as we await the blessed hope
and the coming of our Savior, Jesus Christ.

**For the kingdom,**
**the power and the glory are yours**

**now and for ever.**

***The Rite of Peace***

Lord Jesus Christ, who said to your apostles:
Peace I leave you, my peace I give you,
look not on our sins but on the faith of your Church,
and graciously grant her peace and unity
in accordance with your will.
Who live and reign for ever and ever.

**Amen.**

The peace of the Lord be with you always.

**And with your spirit.**

*The deacon or the priest turns toward the people and adds:*

Let us offer each other the sign of peace.

*All offer one another a sign, in keeping with local custom, that expresses peace, communion, and charity.*

***Breaking of the Bread***

*The priest breaks the host over the paten and places a small piece in the chalice, saying quietly:*

May this mingling of the Body and Blood
of our Lord Jesus Christ
bring eternal life to us who receive it.

*Meanwhile the following is sung or said:*

**Lamb of God, you take away the sins of the world,**
**have mercy on us.**
**Lamb of God, you take away the sins of the world,**
**have mercy on us.**

**Lamb of God, you take away the sins of the world, grant us peace.**

*The invocation may be repeated if the fraction is prolonged. Only the final time, however, is "grant us peace" said.*

***Preparation for Communion***

*The priest, with hands joined, says quietly one of the following:*

1. Lord Jesus Christ, Son of the living God,
who by the will of the Father and the work of the Holy Spirit,
through your death gave life to the world,
free me by this, your most holy Body and Blood,
from all my sins and from every evil;
keep me always faithful to your commandments,
and never let me be parted from you.

*Or*

2. May the receiving of your Body and Blood,
Lord Jesus Christ,
not bring me to judgment and condemnation,
but through your loving mercy
be for me protection in mind and body
and a healing remedy.

*The priest genuflects, takes the host, and holding it slightly raised above the paten or the chalice while facing the people, says aloud:*

Behold the Lamb of God,
behold him who takes away the sins of the world.
Blessed are those called to the supper of the Lamb.

**Lord, I am not worthy**
**that you should enter under my roof,**

**but only say the word**
**and my soul shall be healed.**

*The priest, facing the altar, says quietly:*
May the Body of Christ keep me safe for eternal life.
*And he reverently consumes the Body of Christ.*

*Then he takes the chalice and says quietly:*
May the Blood of Christ keep me safe for eternal life.
*And he reverently consumes the Blood of Christ.*

*The priest and perhaps others distribute Communion. He raises a host slightly, saying:*
The Body of Christ.
*The communicant replies:*
**Amen.**
*If any receive Holy Communion under both kinds:*
The Blood of Christ.
**Amen.**

*After the distribution of Communion, the priest, a deacon, or an acolyte purifies the paten and the chalice.*
*The priest says quietly:*
What has passed our lips as food, O Lord,
may we possess in purity of heart,
that what has been given to us in time
may be our healing for eternity.

***Prayer After Communion***

Let us pray.

*All pray in silence, then the priest says the Prayer After Communion, at the end of which the people acclaim:*

**Amen.**

THE CONCLUDING RITES

The Lord be with you.

**And with your spirit.**

May almighty God bless you,
the Father, and the Son, + and the Holy Spirit.

**Amen.**

*On certain days there is a more solemn formula of blessing or a prayer over the people.*

*The deacon or the priest, with hands joined and facing the people, says:*

Go forth, the Mass is ended.

*Or*

Go and announce the gospel of the Lord.

*Or*

Go in peace, glorifying the Lord by your life.

*Or*

Go in peace.

**Thanks be to God.**

## Prayers After Mass

### *To God the Father*

We thank you, Father, that in this Mass you have accepted our simple gifts of bread and wine and transformed them into the Body and Blood of your well-beloved Son, through the power of your Holy Spirit. Take our lives and transform them, so that we may live as bread that is broken and scattered on the hills to feed our hungry world. We make this prayer through Christ our Lord. Amen.

Michael Buckley

### *To the Holy Spirit*

Spirit of the living God, you have fallen on us afresh at Mass and filled us with your saving grace. May we now, filled with your Spirit, witness to the new life within us and so draw all with whom we come in contact into union with you and so give honor and praise to God our Father. Amen.

Michael Buckley

### *For Sharing the Gospel*

Lord Jesus Christ, you have come to us and shared your life and resurrection with us in this holy Mass; supported by your example and nourished with your Body and Blood, may we share with others the truth of your gospel and the power of your intercession for all mankind. Amen.

Michael Buckley

### *For Peace*

Lord Jesus Christ, at Mass you have given us your peace; show us then the peace we should seek, the peace we must give, the peace we can keep, and the peace we must forgo, so that your life may be lived in us as a sign of your love for everyone to see and experience. Amen.

Michael Buckley

***For the Church***

O God, our refuge and our strength, look down in mercy on your people who cry to you; and by the intercession of the glorious and immaculate virgin Mary, Mother of God, of St. Joseph her spouse, of your blessed apostles Peter and Paul, and of all the saints, in mercy and goodness hear our prayers for the conversion of sinners and for the liberty and exaltation of our holy mother the Church. Through Christ our Lord. Amen.

# THE BLESSED SACRAMENT

**Prayers Before Holy Communion**

***Prayer of St. Thomas Aquinas***

Almighty and ever living God,
I approach the sacrament of your only begotten Son,
our Lord Jesus Christ.
I come sick to the doctor of life,
unclean to the fountain of mercy,
blind to the radiance of eternal light,
and poor and needy to the Lord of heaven and earth.
Lord, in your great generosity,
heal my sickness, wash away my defilement,
enlighten my blindness, enrich my poverty,
and clothe my nakedness.
May I receive the Bread of Angels,
the King of Kings and Lord of Lords,
with humble reverence,
with the purity and faith,
the repentance and love, and the determined purpose
that will help to bring me to salvation.
May I receive the sacrament of the Lord's Body and Blood
and its reality and power.
Kind God,
may I receive the Body of your only begotten Son,
our Lord Jesus Christ,
born from the womb of the Virgin Mary,
and so be received into his mystical body
and numbered among his members.

Loving Father,
as on my earthly pilgrimage
I now receive your beloved Son
under the veil of a sacrament,
may I one day see him face-to-face in glory,
who lives and reigns with you for ever. Amen.

***Prayer of St. Thomas More***

Give me, good Lord, a full faith and a fervent charity,
a love of you, good Lord,
incomparable above the love of myself;
and that I love nothing to your displeasure but
everything in an order to you.
Take from me, good Lord, this lukewarm fashion,
or rather cold manner of meditation
and this dullness in praying to you.
And give me warmth, delight,
and life in thinking about you.
And give me your grace to long for your holy sacraments
and specially to rejoice in the presence of your blessed Body,
sweet Savior Christ, in the holy sacrament of the altar,
and duly to thank you for your gracious coming.

***Prayer of St. Ambrose***

Lord Jesus Christ,
I approach your banquet table
in fear and trembling,
for I am a sinner,
and I dare not rely on my own worth,

but only on your goodness and mercy.
I am defiled by many sins in body and soul
and by my unguarded thoughts and words.

Gracious God of majesty and awe,
I seek your protection;
I look for your healing.
Poor troubled sinner that I am,
I appeal to you, the fountain of all mercy.
I cannot bear your judgment,
but I trust in your salvation.
Lord, I show my wounds to you
and uncover my shame before you.
I know my sins are many and great,
and they fill me with fear,
but I hope in your mercies,
for they cannot be numbered.

Lord Jesus Christ, eternal King, God and man,
crucified for mankind,
look upon me with mercy and hear my prayer,
for I trust in you.
Have mercy on me,
full of sorrow and sin,
for the depth of your compassion never ends.
Praise to you, saving sacrifice,
offered on the wood of the cross for me and for all mankind.
Praise to the noble and precious blood
flowing from the wounds of my crucified Lord Jesus Christ

and washing away the sins of the whole world.
Remember, Lord, your creature,
whom you have redeemed with your blood.
I repent of my sins,
and I long to put right what I have done.

Merciful Father, take away all my offenses and sins;
purify me in body and soul,
and make me worthy to taste the Holy of Holies.
May your Body and Blood,
which I intend to receive, although I am unworthy,
be for me the remission of my sins,
the washing away of my guilt,
the end of my evil thoughts,
and the rebirth of my better instincts.
May it incite me to do the works pleasing to you
and profitable to my health in body and soul,
and be a firm defense
against the wiles of my enemies.
Amen.

***Sancti, venite***

Draw nigh and take the Body of the Lord,
and drink the holy Blood for you outpoured.
Saved by that Body and that holy Blood,
with souls refreshed, we render thanks to God.
Mankind is ransomed from eternal loss
by flesh and blood offered upon the cross.
Salvation's giver, Christ, the only Son,
by his dear cross and blood the victory won.

Offered was he for greatest and for least,
himself the victim, and himself the priest.
Victims are offered by the law of old,
which in a type this heavenly mystery told.
He, ransomer from death and light from shade,
now gives his holy grace, his saints to aid.
Approach ye then with faithful hearts sincere,
and take the safeguard of salvation here.
He, that his saints in this world rules and shields,
to all believers life eternal yields;
With heavenly bread makes them that hunger whole,
gives living waters to the thirsting soul. Amen.

Bangor Antiphonary

***Hail, Sacred Feast***

My God, and is thy table spread,
and does thy cup with love o'erflow?
Thither be all thy children led,
and let them all thy sweetness know.

Hail, sacred feast, which Jesus makes!
Rich banquet of his flesh and blood!
Thrice happy he, who here partakes
that sacred stream, that heavenly food.

O let thy table honored be,
and furnished well with joyful guests;
and may each soul salvation see,
that here its sacred pledges tastes.

Philip Doddridge

### *Act of Faith in the Real Presence*

Lord Jesus Christ, I believe you are as truly present in this holy sacrament, under the signs of bread and wine, as you were when dying upon a cross for the salvation of all mankind, or as you are now enthroned in glory in heaven at the right hand of the Father. You said that you would give us yourself as the Bread of Life; if we eat of it, we shall live forever. I believe this truth because you are truth itself.

With confidence in your loving forgiveness therefore, I approach your altar, conscious that my unworthiness to receive you is outweighed by your desire to be united with my soul. You desire to nourish it on its earthly pilgrimage, until the day when I shall be with you in the eternal banquet, to feed on the unveiled beauty of your presence forever.

### *Prayer to Our Lady*

Most Blessed Virgin Mary, who under the shadow and power of the Holy Spirit prepared in your spotless womb a fit dwelling place for the Incarnate Word of God, intercede for me now so that, by the power of the same Holy Spirit, I may be purified and become less unworthy to receive my Lord and Savior under my roof.

### *Act of Spiritual Communion*

*When unable to receive the sacrament*

My Jesus, I believe that you are truly present in the Most Blessed Sacrament. I love you above all things, and I desire to possess you within my soul. Since I am unable now to receive you sacramentally, come at least spiritually into my heart. I embrace you as if you were already here, and I unite myself wholly to you. Never permit me to be separated from you.

St. Alphonsus

**Prayers After Holy Communion**

***A Hymn of Thanksgiving***

I give you thanks,
Lord, holy Father, everlasting God.
In your great mercy,
and not because of my own merits,
you have fed me, a sinner and your unworthy servant,
with the precious Body and Blood of your Son,
our Lord Jesus Christ.

I pray that this Holy Communion
may not serve as my judgment and condemnation
but as my forgiveness and salvation.

May it be my armor of faith
and shield of good purpose.
May it root out in me all vice and evil desires
and increase my love and patience,
humility and obedience,
and every virtue.

Make it a firm defense
against the wiles of all my enemies, seen and unseen,
while restraining all evil impulses of flesh and spirit.
May it help me cleave to you, the one true God,
and bring me a blessed death when you call.

I beseech you to bring me, a sinner,
to that glorious feast where,
with your Son and Holy Spirit,
you are the true light of your holy ones,
their flawless blessedness,
everlasting joy,
and perfect happiness.
Through Christ our Lord. Amen.

St. Thomas Aquinas

***Prayer Before a Crucifix***

Behold, O kind and most sweet Jesus, I cast myself on my knees in your sight, and with the most fervent desire of my soul, I pray and beseech you that you would impress upon my heart lively sentiments of faith, hope, and charity, with a true repentance for my sins and a firm desire of amendment, while with deep affection and grief of soul I ponder within myself and mentally contemplate your five most precious wounds, having before my eyes that which David spoke in prophecy of you, O good Jesus: "They pierced my hands and my feet; they have numbered all my bones."

***Anima Christi***

Soul of Christ, sanctify me.
Body of Christ, save me.
Blood of Christ, fill me.
Water from the side of Christ, wash me.
Passion of Christ, strengthen me.
O good Jesus, hear me.

Within your wounds hide me.
Suffer me not to be separated from you.
From the malicious enemy defend me.
In the hour of my death call me.
And bid me come unto you.
That with your saints I may praise you.
For ever and ever.

Early Fourteenth-Century Prayer

***For Reverence***

Lord Jesus, who in this wonderful sacrament has left us a memorial of your passion: grant us, we beseech you, so to reverence the sacred mysteries of your Body and Blood that we may always feel in our souls the fruit of your redemption. Who lives and reigns, God, world without end.

***For Closer Union***

Lord Jesus Christ, pierce my soul with your love, so that I may always long for you alone, who are the Bread of Angels and the fulfilment of the soul's deepest desires. May my heart always hunger and feed upon you, so that my soul may be filled with the sweetness of your presence. May my soul thirst for you, who are the source of life, wisdom, knowledge, light, and all the riches of God our Father. May I always seek and find you, think upon you, speak to you, and do all things for the honor and glory of your holy name. Be always my only hope, my peace, my refuge, and my help in whom my heart is rooted so that I may never be separated from you.

St. Bonaventure

### *For the Fruits of the Passion*

Most sweet Jesus Christ, grant that your passion may be to me a power by which I am strengthened, protected, and defended. May your wounds be to me food and drink by which I am nourished and sustained. May the sprinkling of your blood be to me an ablution for all my sins. May your death prove to me life everlasting. and may your cross be to me an eternal glory. May your resurrection be my sure hope of future glory. In these be my refreshment, my joy, my preservation and sweetness of heart.

### *For Mary's Assistance*

Most Holy Mary, with confidence in your intercession, I ask your prayers that I may always have a great devotion to your Son in the Blessed Sacrament and that, as he has given himself to me, so may I dedicate my life to his love and service.

### *For Frequent Reception of Holy Communion*

Loving Lord Jesus, who came into the world to bring the life of grace to those who believe in you, we humbly ask you to pour upon us all the gifts of the Holy Spirit. May those who have neglected you turn to you and long to receive you in Holy Communion, and may we who today received your Body and Blood learn to approach your sacred banquet daily with devotion. There we will receive the remedy for all our faults and be so nourished with the life of your grace that we may come at last to the happiness of life with you at your eternal banquet.

## Prayers Before the Blessed Sacrament

### *Prayer to Begin Eucharistic Adoration*

Loving Father, your beloved Son has told us, "No one can come to me unless the Father who sent me draw him" (John 6:44). Thank you for drawing me here to the Eucharistic presence of Christ your Son. Thank you for allowing me to come close to the One who has come close to us in the Eucharist—who has become our companion on the way to you. Accept my sacrifice of prayer and the adoration I offer to your Son in the Blessed Sacrament. Unworthy though I am, I come to behold Jesus Christ in the Sacrament of Charity, moved by the certainty that anyone who sees Jesus sees the Father. What impels me to this place is the same hunger that sent the starving Prodigal Son back to the embrace of his father. I come begging for a new beginning. Like those present at the feeding of the five thousand, I have nothing to offer you except my nothingness. But I look to your Son and join him in the thanks he offers to you. I come before the presence of your Son filled with an attitude of expectation. All my life, my heart has cried out with the psalmist, "Lower your heavens and come down!" (see Psalm 144:5). With unimaginable mercy you have answered that plea. I have been made for this presence. May I never be without wonder before the miracle of Jesus present in the Eucharist. Let me relive the surprise of the attraction of Christ. Give me eyes to see beyond all appearances. Make me attentive to the encounter you offer me in this Sacrament. Please help me to offer this time of adoration with all my heart, without becoming weary or distracted. United with the Mother of God, may I ardently adore the Fruit of Mary's womb so that my life may become fruitful in the way that best pleases you and that gives you unending glory. I ask this in the name of Jesus Christ the Lord. Amen.

Fr. Peter John Cameron, O.P.

***Prayer of Love for a Holy Hour***

Most sweet Jesus, I believe that you are as truly present here in the tabernacle as when you walked in Galilee, where you ministered to the sick, the lame, and the blind. Your ears of mercy were ever open to listen to the cries of the sorrowing and wounded, and your lips ever ready to speak words of sympathy, comfort, and encouragement to those who trusted in your power to help them.

As a sinner conscious of your mercy, I come before you now to spend an hour in communion with you. Too long have I heard your plea, "Could you not watch one hour?" (Mark 14:37), and too long have I neglected to respond to it. Now at last I come to you, Jesus, my patient and faithful friend, to whom I can open my heart as someone who fully understands me.

Sweet Jesus, you know me better than I know myself. You perceive the innermost secrets of my heart and see there my longing to be totally yours. Deep down within me I want to love you, but at the same time I am aware of the promptings of my sinful nature drawing me away from you and the unselfish service that I should render you. Jesus, I have asked, and now ask you again, to make me love you in spite of my weaker self. Fill each day of my life with acts of love for you, and make me realize what your love really means. Enlighten my understanding, that I may clearly see that to love you means wealth beyond measure, and to serve you reward without limit. Sweet heart of Jesus, I implore that I may love you daily more and more.

***Adoro te devote***

Godhead here in hiding, whom I do adore,
Masked by these bare shadows, shape and nothing more,
See, Lord, at thy service low lies here a heart
Lost, all lost in wonder, at the God thou art.

Seeing, touching, tasting are in thee deceived;
How says trusty hearing? That shall be believed;
What God's Son has told me, take for truth I do;
Truth himself speaks truly, or there's nothing true.

On the cross thy Godhead made no sign to men;
Here thy very manhood steals from human ken:
Both are my confession, both are my belief,
And I pray the prayer of the dying thief.

I am not like Thomas, wounds I cannot see,
But can plainly call thee Lord and God as he.
This faith each day deeper be my holding of,
Daily make me harder hope and dearer love.

O thou our reminder of Christ crucified,
Living Bread the life of us for whom he died,
Lend this life to me then: Feed and feast my mind,

There be thou the sweetness man was meant to find.

Bring the tender tale true of the pelican;
Bathe me, Jesu Lord, in what thy bosom ran—
Blood that but one drop of has the worth to win
All the world forgiveness of its world of sin.
Jesu, whom I look at shrouded here below,
I beseech thee send me what I thirst for so,
Some day to gaze on thee face-to-face in light
And be blest for ever with thy glory's sight.
St. Thomas Aquinas, translated by Gerard Manley Hopkins

***To Be With You in Silence***

In silence
To be there before you, Lord, that's all,
To shut the eyes of my body,
To shut the eyes of my soul,
And to be still and silent,
To expose myself to you who are there, exposed to me.
To be there before you, the Eternal Presence.
I am willing to feel nothing, Lord,
    to see nothing,
    to hear nothing.
Empty of all ideas,
    of all images,
In the darkness.
Here I am, simply
To meet you without obstacles,

In the silence of faith,
Before you, Lord.

Michel Quoist

***Sweet Heart of Jesus***

Sweet heart of Jesus,
  fount of love and mercy,
today we come,
  thy blessing to implore;
O touch our hearts,
  so cold and so ungrateful,
and make them, Lord,
  thine own for evermore.

Sweet heart of Jesus, we implore,
O make us love thee more and more.

Sweet heart of Jesus,
  make us know and love thee,
unfold to us
  the treasures of thy grace;
that so our hearts,
  from things of earth uplifted,
may long alone
  to gaze upon thy face.

Sweet heart of Jesus,
  make us pure and gentle,
and teach us how
  to do thy blessed will;

to follow close
  the print of thy dear footsteps,
and when we fall,
  sweet heart, oh, love us still.

Sweet heart of Jesus,
  bless all hearts that love thee,
and may thine own
  heart ever blessed be;
bless us, dear Lord,
  and bless the friends we cherish,
and keep us true
  to Mary and to thee.

Traditional

***Seeking a Blessing***

My Jesus, take from my heart all that displeases you, and bless me as you blessed your disciples before ascending into heaven. May this blessing change me, fill me with your Holy Spirit, and be an assured pledge of the final benediction that you will bestow on me and all your elect on the Last Day.

***Food for Service***

O Jesus, present in the sacrament of the altar, teach all the nations to serve you with willing hearts, knowing that to serve God is to reign. May your sacrament, O Jesus, be light to the mind, strength to the will, joy to the heart. May it be the support of the weak, the comfort of the suffering, the wayfaring bread of salvation for the dying, and for all the pledge of future glory.

Pope John XXIII

### *For Families in Need*

O Living Bread that came down from heaven to give life to the world! O loving Shepherd of our souls, from your throne of glory whence, a "hidden God," you pour out your grace on families and peoples, we commend to you particularly the sick, the unhappy, the poor, and all who beg for food and employment, imploring for all and every one the assistance of your providence; we commend to you the families, so that they may be fruitful centers of Christian life. May the abundance of your grace be poured out over all.

Pope John XXIII

### *Act of Consecration*

Lord Jesus Christ, who for love of us remains night and day in this sacrament, full of kindness and love, awaiting, inviting, and welcoming all who come to visit you: I believe that you are present in the sacrament of the altar. I adore you from the depth of my own nothingness, and I thank you for all the graces that you have granted me. I thank you especially for having given yourself to me in this sacrament; for having given me your own most holy mother, Mary, for my advocate; and for having called me to visit you in this church. I pay homage this day to your adorable heart and desire to do so for three ends: first, in thanksgiving for this great gift; second, to make reparation for all the injuries you have received in this sacrament from your enemies; and third, to adore you, through this visit, in all the places on earth where your sacramental presence is least honored and most neglected.

My Jesus, I love you with my whole heart. I am sorry for having offended your infinite goodness so many times in the past. I resolve, with the help of your grace, never to offend you again; and at this present moment I consecrate myself completely to you. I give to you, withholding nothing, all my own will, my inclinations, my desires, everything that is mine. From this day forward, do with me and with what belongs to me as it shall please you. All that I ask and desire is your holy love, final perseverance, and the perfect fulfillment of your will. I commend to you the souls in purgatory, particularly those who were most devoted to the Blessed Sacrament and to Mary, your holy mother. I commend to you too all poor sinners.

And now, dear Savior, I join all my desires with the desires of your loving heart; I offer them to your eternal Father, and I beg him in your name, and for your love, to accept them and fulfill them.

***Paul's Prayer***

I bow my knees before the Father, from whom every family in heaven and on earth is named, that according to the riches of his glory he may grant you to be strengthened with might through his Spirit in the inner man, and that Christ may dwell in your hearts through faith; that you, being rooted and grounded in love, may have power to comprehend with all the saints what is the breadth and length and height and depth, and to know the love of Christ which surpasses knowledge, that you may be filled with all the fullness of God.

Now to him who by the power at work within us is able to do far more abundantly than all that we ask or think, to him be glory in the Church and in Christ Jesus to all generations, for ever and ever. Amen.

Ephesians 3:14–21

***Sweet Sacrament***

Jesus, my Lord, my God, my all,
how can I love thee as I ought?
And how revere this wondrous gift,
so far surpassing hope or thought?

Sweet Sacrament, we thee adore;
Oh, make us love thee more and more.

Had I but Mary's sinless heart
to love thee with, my dearest King,
Oh, with what bursts of fervent praise
thy goodness, Jesus, would I sing!

Ah, see! within a creature's hand
the vast Creator deigns to be,
reposing, infant-like, as though
on Joseph's arm or Mary's knee.

Thy body, soul, and Godhead, all;
O mystery of love divine!
I cannot compass all I have,
for all thou hast and art are mine.

Sound, sound, his praises higher still,
and come, ye angels, to our aid;

'tis God, 'tis God, the very God
whose power both man and angels made.

Frederick William Faber

### *Act of Trust*

Lord Jesus, I believe in your presence on the altar; help my unbelief. I trust my life to you; fill up my lack of confidence. I love you: Warm my cold heart, which seeks comfort elsewhere. Accept my faith, hope, and love such as they are, and through the power of your sacred presence, make up for what is lacking so that I may know, trust, and serve you this and every day of my life.

### *Act of Love*

You know better than I how much I love you, Lord. You know it and I know it not, for nothing is more hidden from me than the depths of my own heart. I desire to love you; I fear that I do not love you enough. I beseech you to grant me the fullness of pure love. Behold my desire; you have given it to me. Behold in your creature what you have placed there. O God, who love me enough to inspire me to love you for ever, behold not my sins. Behold your mercy and my love.

### *For the Fullness of Love*

Set our hearts on fire with love for you, O Christ our God, that in that flame we may love you with all our hearts, with all our minds, with all our souls, and with all our strength, and our neighbors as ourselves; so that, keeping your commandments, we may glorify you, the giver of all good gifts.

### *Prayer of Abandonment*

Be a light to my eyes, music to my ears, sweetness to my taste, and full contentment to my heart. Be my sunshine in the day, my food at table, my repose in the night, my clothing in nakedness, and my succor in all necessities. Lord Jesu, I give you my body, my soul, my substance, my frame, my friends, my liberty, and my life. Dispose of me and all that is mine as it may seem best to you and to the glory of your blessed name. Amen.

### *A Light to Others*

My Lord and my God,
thank you for drawing me to yourself.
Make me desire more deeply
that knowledge of you that is eternal life.
Lord, you have told us that the pure in heart shall see God
—the single-minded who do not try to serve two masters,
who have no other gods but you.
Keep the burning of my desire for you
as clear and steady as the flame of a candle
—a single, undivided focus of attention,
a steady offering of the will.
Let my whole being be filled with your light,
so that others may be drawn to you.
Let my whole being be cleansed
by the flame of your love
from all that is contrary to your will for me,
from all that keeps others from coming to you.
Let my whole being be consumed in your service,

so that others may know your love,
my Lord and my God.

***An Instrument of Love***

Use me, my Savior, for whatever purpose and in whatever way you may require. Here is my poor heart, an empty vessel; fill it with your grace. Here is my sinful, troubled soul; quicken it and refresh it with your love. Take my heart for your abode; my mouth to spread abroad the glory of your name; my love and all my powers for the advancement of your believing people, and never suffer the steadfastness and confidence of my faith to abate.

***For the Conversion of Sinners***

Most Holy Trinity, Father, Son and Holy Spirit, I adore you profoundly, and I offer you the most precious Body, Blood, soul, and divinity of Jesus Christ, present in all the tabernacles of the world, in reparation for the outrages, sacrileges, and indifferences with which he is offended; and by the infinite merits of his most Sacred Heart and of the Immaculate Heart of Mary, I ask you for the conversion of all sinners.

***Aspirations***

My Lord and my God.

O sacrament most holy, O sacrament divine,
All praise and all thanksgiving be every moment thine.

O heart of Jesus in the Blessed Sacrament, burning with love for us, inflame our hearts with love for thee.

May the heart of Jesus in the Most Blessed Sacrament be praised, adored, and loved, with grateful affection at every moment, in all the tabernacles of the world, even to the end of time.

My Jesus, I adore you present on the altar for love of me: grant that I may love you more and more.

My Jesus, I thank you with all my heart for your loving kindness to me. Blessed and praised every moment be the most holy and divine Sacrament.

My Jesus, in the Most Holy Sacrament you have given yourself to me: Accept in return all the senses of my body and all the faculties of my soul. Give me light and grace: light to know your holy will and grace to do it.

Lord Jesus, I give you my body, my soul, my possessions and friends, all that I am and have. Dispose of them according to your will and to the glory of your name.

My Jesus, too often have I offended you, and now before you in the Blessed Sacrament I ask the grace never to sin again.

**Eucharistic Exposition**

***O Salutaris Hostia***

O salutaris hostia,
Quae caeli pandis ostium;
Bella premunt hostilia,
Da robur, fer auxilium.

Uni Trinoque Domino
Sit sempiterna gloria,
Qui vitam sine termino
Nobis donet in patria.
Amen.

*Or*

***O Saving Victim***

O saving victim, opening wide
the gate of heaven to man below;
our foes press on from every side;
your aid supply, your strength bestow.

To your great name be endless praise,
immortal Godhead, one in three;
O grant us endless length of days
in our true native land with thee. Amen.

**Eucharistic Benediction**

***Tantum Ergo***

Tantum ergo Sacramentum
Veneremur cernui:
Et antiquum documentum
Novo cedat ritui:
Praestet fides supplementum
Sensuum defectui.

Genitori, Genitoque
Laus et jubilatio,
Salus, honor, virtus quoque
Sit et benedictio;
Procedenti ab utroque
Compar sit laudatio.
Amen.

*Or*

***Humbly Let Us Voice Our Homage***

Therefore we, before him bending,
this great sacrament revere;
types and shadows have their ending,
for the newer rite is here;
faith our outward sense befriending,
makes the inward vision clear.

Glory let us give, and blessing
to the Father and the Son;
honor, might, and praise addressing,
while eternal ages run;
ever too his love confessing,
who, from both, with both is one.
Amen.

*The minister may lead the faithful in one or more of the following prayers:*

For your gift of the Eucharist,
through which we proclaim the Lord's death until he comes again:

God, Our Father, we bless you.

For the gift of the Eucharist,
through which you give us strength and satisfy our hunger:

God, Our Father, we bless you.

For your gift of the Eucharist,
through which all your children are brought together in brotherly love:

God, Our Father, we bless you.

You are the Bread of Life:

Praise to you.

You are the Bread of Salvation:

Praise to you.

You are the Blood that redeemed us:

Praise to you.

You are the source of our joy:

Praise to you.

You are the Bread that feeds us:

Praise to you.

You are the Blood that quenches our thirst:

Praise to you.

You are the Bread that comforts us:

Praise to you.

You are the Bread that gives us strength:

Praise to you.

You are the Bread that heals us in body and mind:

Praise to you.

Lord Jesus Christ,
you gave us the Eucharist
as the memorial of your suffering and death.
May our worship of this sacrament of your Body and Blood
help us to experience the salvation you won for us
and the peace of the kingdom,
where you live with the Father and the Holy Spirit,
one God, for ever and ever.

Amen.

*Or*

Lord our God,
in this great sacrament
we come into the presence of Jesus Christ, your Son,
born of the virgin Mary
and crucified for our salvation.
May we who declare our faith in this fountain of love and mercy
drink from it the water of everlasting life.

Amen.

*Or*

Lord our God,
may we always give due honor
to the sacramental presence of the Lamb who was slain for us.
May our faith be rewarded
by the vision of his glory,
who lives and reigns for ever and ever.

Amen.

*Or*

Lord our God,
you have given us the true Bread from heaven.
In the strength of this food,
may we live always by your life
and rise in glory on the last day.

Amen.

*Or*

Lord, give to our hearts
the light of faith and the fire of love,
that we may worship in spirit and in truth
our God and Lord, present in this sacrament,
who lives and reigns for ever and ever.
Amen.

*Or*

Lord, may this sacrament of new life
warm our hearts with your love
and make us eager
for the eternal joy of your kingdom.
Amen.

*Or*

Lord our God,
teach us to cherish in our hearts
the paschal mystery of your Son,
by which you redeemed the world.
Watch over the gifts of grace
your love has given us
and bring them to fulfillment
in the glory of heaven.
Amen.

***The Divine Praises***

Blessed be God.
Blessed be His Holy Name.
Blessed be Jesus Christ, true God and true Man.

Blessed be the Name of Jesus.
Blessed be His Most Sacred Heart.
Blessed be His Most Precious Blood.
Blessed be Jesus in the Most Holy Sacrament of the Altar.
Blessed be the Holy Spirit, the Paraclete.
Blessed be the great Mother of God, Mary most Holy.
Blessed be her Holy and Immaculate Conception.
Blessed be her Glorious Assumption.
Blessed be the name of Mary, Virgin and Mother.
Blessed be St. Joseph, her most chaste spouse.
Blessed be God in His Angels and in His Saints. Amen.

***Adoremus***

Adoremus in aeternum sanctissimum Sacramentum.
Laudate Dominum, omnes gentes;
laudate eum omnes populi.

Quoniam confirmata est super nos misericordia ejus;
et veritas Domini manet in aeternum.

Gloria Patri, et Filio,
et Spiritui Sancto.
Sicut erat in principio, et nunc, et semper,
et in saecula saeculorum. Amen.
Adoremus in aeternum sanctissimum Sacramentum.

*Or*

***Let Us Adore***

Let us adore for ever the most holy Sacrament.
O praise the Lord, all you nations;

praise him, all you people.

For his mercy is confirmed upon us;
and the truth of the Lord remains for ever.

Glory be to the Father, and to the Son,
and to the Holy Spirit.
As it was in the beginning, is now,
and ever shall be, world without end. Amen.
Let us adore for ever the most holy Sacrament.

## RECONCILIATION

*Jesus Christ is the reconciler between us and God. By his wounds we are healed, when through sin we stray from the path that leads to union with God our Father:* "In Christ God was reconciling the world to himself, not counting their trespasses against them" (2 Corinthians 5:19).

*Just as the Eucharist is the most perfect form of the celebration of our loving union with God in Christ, so the sacrament of reconciliation is the most privileged form of Christ's forgiving us our offenses against God, our neighbor, and ourselves.*

We give and receive forgiveness within the Church, as members of Christ's body; so in common with all the sacraments, reconciliation is essentially a "Church" sacrament. It is a community action. While individual confession is still required, nevertheless the Christian community dimension is never forgotten. When we sin the whole body suffers; when we repent and are reconciled, the whole body increases in holiness and grace. We are not alone in sinning or in being reconciled.

In order to understand this sacrament, we need to appreciate the three-dimensional nature of sin. Sin divides us from God, separates us from each other, and sets up a conflict within ourselves as individuals.

1. *Alienation from God.* Sin means that we refuse to give our Father the loving obedience that is his due.

2. *Division among people.* Every sin harms the community, at least indirectly, in that it introduces disorder into people's attitudes and conduct.

3. *Disintegration of the individual.* Sin disturbs the balance between the two poles—love of God and our neighbor—that should direct our lives.

If sin is abandoning the Father's house, then repentance is returning to it. The mission of Christ and the Church is a mission of repentance. *Repent and believe the gospel* is the keynote and driving force of the sacrament of reconciliation. The reading of God's Word in the celebration of the sacrament calls forth our response, by which we are healed and reconciled. Reconciliation is a gospel- and community-based sacrament.

The three aspects of repentance cancel out the three-dimensional nature of our sin.

1. *Conversion to God.* We admit our sin, recognize we are not worthy of God's love, and trusting in the merits of Christ, throw ourselves on the mercy of God.
2. *Reconciliation with the community.* We return in love and reparation to the community we have offended.
3. *Integration of self.* Conversion gradually purifies us so that we may more perfectly love God and our neighbor as ourselves.

The sacrament of reconciliation is frequently celebrated in the community setting of penitential services. In every celebration, whether individual or collective, Christ's reconciling, healing power is at work in the Church.

## Prayers Before Receiving the Sacrament of Reconciliation

### *To God the Father*

Almighty and most merciful God, who made me out of nothing and redeemed me by the precious blood of your only Son, I humbly ask you to forgive my sins. I desire most sincerely to forsake all my evil ways in which I have lost my true self. With the Prodigal Son in the gospel story, I desire to think seriously about the direction of my life, and like him I resolve to return to my Father's house even though I am not worthy to be called your child. I know that you desire the conversion of the sinner and that your mercy is above all your works. It is in this mercy that I place my trust, and as you have spared me so long and given me the desire of returning to you, so may you finish the work you have begun and bring me to full and perfect reconciliation with you.

I desire now to confess sincerely all my sins to you and your priest, and for this purpose I wish to know myself and call myself to account by a diligent examination of my conscience. But what will it avail to know my sins if you do not also give me the grace of sorrow and repentance? You insist on a change of heart, without which there can be no reconciliation, and it is you alone who can bring about this change in me. Grant me, Father, this change of heart, as well as a lively faith and firm hope in the saving passion of your Son. I ask this through Christ, our Lord. Amen.

### *To God the Son*

Lord Jesus Christ, in your great love you wish that every sinner be converted and live in your grace. I grieve from the bottom of my heart that by my sins I have offended you, who shed your blood for me. May the same blood now plead for mercy for me before the face of God, our Father. For love of you I forgive all who have offended me, and I firmly resolve to forsake every occasion of sin. I now sorrowfully confess all the sins I have committed against your divine goodness.

***To God the Holy Spirit***

Come, Holy Spirit, fill my heart with an awareness of your presence, and kindle in me the fire of your love. Help me to discover my sins of commission and omission by which I have offended you and my neighbor. May I confess them with a humble and contrite heart, and by the help of your grace may I never sin again.

***For True Sorrow***

O sweet Jesus, I grieve for my sins; vouchsafe to supply whatever is lacking to my true sorrow and to offer for me to God the Father all the grief that thou hast endured because of my sins and those of the whole world.

St. Mechtilde

O Jesus, you who had no pity on yourself, you who are God, have pity on me who am a sinner.

Pierre Barbet

***For the Intercession of Our Lady***

Holy virgin, mother of our Lord Jesus Christ, compassionate refuge of penitent sinners, by the sacred wounds of your Son and the agony you felt as you stood by the foot of the cross, intercede for me now so that, sorrowful for my sins, I may humbly confess them and live with your Son the life of the Resurrection.

***For the Aid of My Guardian Angel and All the Saints***

O guardian angel, sent to watch over me during my life, be with me now in my sorrow for my sins. May my holy patron N., whose name I bear, St. Peter, St. Mary Magdalene, and all the saints be my cloud of witnesses before the throne of God, so that like the Prodigal Son, I may return to my Father's house, never to leave it again.

***From the Penitential Psalms***

*It is a pious custom to recite the seven penitential psalms as prayers against the seven deadly sins.*

O Lord, rebuke me not in your anger,
  nor chasten me in your wrath.
Have mercy on me, O Lord, for I am languishing;
  O Lord, heal me, for my bones are troubled.
My soul also is sorely troubled.

Psalm 6:1–3

Blessed is he whose transgression is forgiven,
  whose sin is covered.
. . .
I acknowledged my sin to you,
  and I did not hide my iniquity;
I said, "I will confess my transgressions to the Lord."
then you forgave the guilt of my sin.

Psalm 32:1, 5

My wounds grow foul and fester
because of my foolishness,
I am utterly bowed down and prostrate;
all the day I go about mourning.
…
Lord, all my longing is known to you,
my sighing is not hidden from you.

Psalm 38:5–6, 9

Have mercy on me, O God, according to your merciful love;
according to your abundant mercy blot out my transgressions.
Wash me thoroughly from my iniquity,
and cleanse me from my sin!
For I know my transgressions,
and my sin is ever before me.
Against you, you only, have I sinned,
and done that which is evil in your sight.
…
Purge me with hyssop, and I shall be clean;
wash me, and I shall be whiter than snow.

Psalm 51:1–4, 7

Hear my prayer, O Lord,
let my cry come to you!
Do not hide your face from me
in the day of my distress!
Incline your ear to me;
answer me speedily in the day when I call!

For my days pass away like smoke,…
My heart is struck down like grass, and withered.

Psalm 102:1–3, 4

Out of the depths I cry to you, O Lord!
  Lord, hear my voice!
Let your ears be attentive
  to the voice of my supplications!

If you, O Lord, should mark iniquities,
  Lord, who could stand?
But there is forgiveness with you,
  that you may be feared.

Psalm 130:1–4

…In your faithfulness answer me, in your righteousness!
Enter not into judgment with your servant;
  for no man living is righteous before you.
…
For your name's sake, O Lord, preserve my life!
  In your righteousness bring me out of trouble!

Psalm 143:1–2, 11

***Before Examination of Conscience***

Lord Jesus Christ, judge of the living and the dead, before whom I must appear one day to give an exact account of my whole life, enlighten me, I beseech you, and give me a humble and contrite heart, that I may see where I have offended your infinite majesty and judge myself now with such a just severity that then you may judge me with mercy and clemency.

*After Examination of Conscience*

My God, I detest these and all other sins that I have committed against your divine majesty. I am sorry that I have offended you, because you are infinitely good and sin displeases you. I love you with my whole heart, and I firmly purpose, by the help of your grace, never more to offend you. I resolve to avoid the occasions of sin; I will confess my sins and endeavor to make satisfaction for them. Have mercy on me, O God, have mercy, and pardon me, a wretched sinner. In the name of your beloved Son, Jesus, I humbly beg you to wash me with his precious blood, so that my sins may be entirely remitted.

**Prayers After Receiving the Sacrament of Reconciliation**

***To God the Father***

Almighty and merciful God, I thank you that once again you have welcomed me, your prodigal child, despite the many times I have strayed from you. Because of your tender mercies, I now offer the rest of my life to your service and renounce with my whole soul all the offenses I have committed against you. I renew my baptismal promises and ask your grace, that in the future I may remain close to you, never to leave you again.

***To God the Son***

Incarnate Word of God, who in your flesh reconciled all men to the Father and continue to reconcile all those who in heart-felt sorrow confess their sins, I thank you that your healing power has touched me and cleansed me from the leprosy of sin. Mercifully direct all my thoughts, words, and actions to the greater glory of the Father, and be my model and help for the rest of my life, so that I may persevere in your service and love.

### *To God the Holy Spirit*

Holy Spirit, under whose guidance and inspiration I have confessed my sins, supply in me whatever is lacking in sorrow for my sins or purity of intention. Grant that the absolution pronounced on earth may be ratified in heaven, so that confident of your dwelling in me as in a holy temple, I may never defile it again but use it as a house of prayer, thanksgiving, and service.

### *Through Our Lady, My Guardian Angel, and All the Saints*

O blessed Mary, my guardian angel and patron saint, St. N., and all the saints, give glory on my behalf to the blessed Trinity, "for he who is mighty has done great things for me, and holy is his name" (Luke 1:49). Intercede for me before God's throne, so that when temptations come in the future, I may not dispute or compromise with them but reject them absolutely, lest I put the Lord our God to the test. May I be counted one day among the blessed in heaven, so that together with you I may praise God for his surpassing compassion and love.

### *In Thanksgiving*

Bless the LORD, O my soul;
  and all that is within me, bless his holy name!
Bless the LORD, O my soul,
  and forget not all his benefits,

who forgives all your iniquity,
  who heals all your diseases,
who redeems your life from the Pit,
  who crowns you with mercy and compassion,
who satisfies you with good as long as you live
  so that your youth is renewed like the eagle's.

Psalm 103:1–5

# A LIFE OF PRAYER

Prayer is our birthright as Christians. It is God's gift to us, and it should be as "natural" to us as breathing. All Christian prayer is identified with the risen Christ, who in himself and for us has conquered sin, death, and the power of the world over us. Since Christ prays through us, we never pray alone, because Christ's Spirit is one with our spirit. This is so because through baptism we are united with the risen Lord, and by his Spirit we call God *Abba, Father!* (Romans 8:15). His Spirit is one with ours. Prayer is therefore a loving relationship between God the Father and us. It is in the truest sense of the word a conversation between God within us and God around us. And all because Christ prays in us to his Father.

We believe that God is more ready to listen to us than we are to speak to him, ready to give infinitely more than we can ask or imagine. So we are truly praying when we listen to what he is saying to us in people, places, and situations. Nothing is outside his love for us, even if our life entails suffering and death. The deepest prayer, therefore, is born of creative silence, when God speaks to us of his will for our lives and its fulfillment.

There are some deep emotions of the Spirit that defy verbal expression: "Likewise the Spirit helps us in our weakness; for we do not choose words in order to pray properly, the Spirit himself expresses our plea in a way that could never be put into words, and God who knows everything in our hearts knows perfectly well what he means" (Romans 8:26–27).

Prayer is as varied and colorful as a rainbow. We may pray privately or in groups. From the earliest days of the Church, the disciples of Jesus, as a group, would pray, as was the Jewish custom, at certain hours of the day: They went as a body to the temple every day (see Acts 2:46).

Christ also said: "But when you pray, go into your room and shut the door and pray to your Father who is in secret, and your Father who sees in secret will reward you" (Matthew 6:6). There is no substitute for personal prayer, which bears the stamp of our individual and unique relationship with God. We may use set prayers, or we might prefer to speak spontaneously, as the Spirit moves us. What is important is that our prayers are born of the Spirit.

Prayer, even though dynamic and often defying analysis, is generally divided up into five categories: invocation, confession, thanksgiving, petition, and intercession.

- Invocation: We not only call God to be present to us but also remind ourselves that God is always present to us when we call on his name.
- Confession: We tell God of our sins of commission and omission.
- Thanksgiving: We praise and thank God for his goodness in creation and redemption.
- Petition: We ask God for the things we need for our life.
- Intercession: We bring the wider needs of the Church and the world to God, who will provide for them.

All these forms of prayer, especially thanksgiving, are found in the Mass. The Spirit of the risen Christ takes all our prayers and offers them to the Father. In prayer we surrender our lives to his loving care. We can do nothing greater.

Because as Christians we are one in and with Christ through baptism, we are also in spiritual communion with each other. We belong to the communion of saints, which embraces all those who are part of Christ's Church, irrespective of time and space. The mother of Christ, the apostles, and all the holy men and women who, down through the ages, kept the flame of faith burning are the great cloud of witnesses on every side of us (see Hebrews 12:1), who encourage us in our struggle on earth. We honor them because of their faithfulness to the gospel and because, in a special way, they are God's friends. They are part of our unseen community, who join us in our prayers through Jesus Christ, his Son. Where they are, one day we hope to be, when we will join them and the angels in one triumphant hymn of praise to God our loving Father.

# DAILY PRAYERS

*We should* "pray constantly" *(1 Thessalonians 5:17), so that* waking we may watch with Christ and sleeping we may rest in peace. *With minds and hearts fixed constantly on God, everything in our lives, whether in action or repose, is a hymn of praise and prayer. We may use reflection, aspirations, formal or spontaneous prayer as the Spirit moves us. All will be to the Father's glory.*

**General Prayers**

***The Lord's Prayer***

Our Father, who art in heaven,
hallowed be thy name;
thy kingdom come;
thy will be done on earth as it is in heaven.
Give us this day our daily bread;
and forgive us our trespasses,
as we forgive those who trespass against us;
and lead us not into temptation,
but deliver us from evil.
Amen.

***The Hail Mary***

Hail Mary, full of grace,
the Lord is with thee.
Blessed art thou among women,
and blessed is the fruit of thy womb, Jesus.
Holy Mary, Mother of God,
pray for us sinners, now

and at the hour of our death.
Amen.

### *The Doxology*

Glory be to the Father,
and to the Son,
and to the Holy Spirit.
As it was in the beginning,
is now, and ever shall be,
world without end.
Amen.

### *The Apostles' Creed*

I believe in God, the Father almighty, Creator of heaven and earth, and in Jesus Christ, his only Son, our Lord, who was conceived by the Holy Spirit, born of the Virgin Mary, suffered under Pontius Pilate, was crucified, died, and was buried; he descended into hell; on the third day he rose again from the dead; he ascended into heaven and is seated at the right hand of God the Father almighty; from there he will come to judge the living and the dead. I believe in the Holy Spirit, the holy catholic Church, the communion of saints, the forgiveness of sins, the resurrection of the body, and life everlasting. Amen.

### *Act of Contrition*

O my God, I am sorry and beg pardon for all my sins, and I detest them above all things, because they deserve your dreadful punishments, because they have crucified my loving Savior Jesus Christ, and most of all, because they offend your infinite goodness; and I firmly resolve, by the help of your grace, never to offend you again and carefully to avoid the occasions of sin. Amen.

### *Prayer Before the Acts*

O almighty and eternal God, grant us an increase of faith, hope, and charity. May we obtain what you have promised, loving and practicing what you command, through Jesus Christ our Lord. Amen.

### *Act of Faith*

O my God, I firmly believe that you are the one only God, the Creator and sovereign Lord of heaven and earth, infinitely great and infinitely good. I firmly believe that in you, one only God, there are three Divine Persons, really distinct and equal in all things, the Father, the Son, and the Holy Spirit. I firmly believe that Jesus Christ, God the Son, became man; that he was conceived by the Holy Spirit and was born of the Virgin Mary; that he suffered and died on the cross to redeem and save us; that he arose the third day from the dead; that he ascended into heaven; that he will come at the end of the world to judge mankind; and that he will reward the good with eternal happiness and condemn the wicked to the everlasting pains of hell. I believe these and all other articles that the holy Roman Catholic Church proposes to our belief, because you, my God, the infallible truth, revealed them and have commanded us to hear the Church, which is the pillar and the ground of truth. In this faith I am firmly resolved, by your holy grace, to live and die. Amen.

*Act of Hope*

My God, you have graciously promised every blessing, even heaven itself, through Jesus Christ to those who keep your commandments. Relying on your infinite power, goodness, and mercy, and confiding in your sacred promises, to which you are always faithful, I confidently hope to obtain pardon of all my sins; grace to serve you faithfully in this life, by doing the good works you have commanded, which, with your assistance, I will perform; and eternal happiness in the next, through my Lord and Savior Jesus Christ. Amen.

*Act of Charity*

My God, I love you with my whole heart and soul and above all things, because you are infinitely good and perfect and most worthy of all my love; and for your sake I love my neighbor as myself. Mercifully grant, O my God, that having loved you on earth, I may love and enjoy you for ever in heaven. Amen.

**Short Acts**

*Act of Faith*

O God, I firmly believe all the truths that you have revealed and that you teach us through your Church, for you are truth itself and can neither deceive nor be deceived.

*Act of Hope*

O God, I hope with complete trust that you will give me, through the merits of Jesus Christ, all necessary grace in this world and everlasting life in the world to come, for this is what you have promised, and you always keep your promises.

*Act of Charity*

O God, I love you with my whole heart above all things, because you are infinitely good; and for your sake I love my neighbor as I love myself.

*Act of Contrition*

O God, I am sorry with my whole heart for all my sins, because you are goodness itself and sin is an offense against you. Therefore I firmly resolve, with the help of your grace, not to sin again and to avoid the occasions of sin.

**At the Day's Beginning**

***To the Holy Trinity***

Most Holy Trinity, your goodness has brought me to the beginning of this day, and now I offer it to you with its thoughts, words, and actions, together with any crosses and contradictions I may encounter. Give your blessing to this day, your gift to me, so that it may be animated with your love and so bring glory and honor to your divine majesty. Amen.

Glory be to the Father, who when I did not exist created me by his power in the likeness of his own image; and to the Son, who when I was lost redeemed me by his precious blood; and to the Holy Spirit, who by his grace and goodness justified me in baptism and many times afterward when I had fallen. For each and all these benefits, be the glory as great as it was in the beginning, and still greater be now in the course of this present life, and ever shall be to the consummation of the world and world without end. Amen.

As I recite this doxology, I wish to offer to the Holy Trinity all praise, and I shall endeavor by grace to live this praise in action throughout this day and for the rest of my life.

***To God the Father***

Father,
I abandon myself into your hands;
do with me what you will.
Whatever you may do I thank you:
I am ready for all; I accept all.

Let only your will be done in me
and in all your creatures.
I wish no more than this, O Lord.

Into your hands I commend my soul:
I offer it to you
with all the love of my heart,
for I love you, Lord,
and so need to give myself,
to surrender myself into your hands,
without reserve
and with boundless confidence,
for you are my Father.

Charles de Foucauld

***We Commend Our Day***

Into your hands, O Lord, we commend ourselves this day. Let your presence be with us to its close. Strengthen us to remember that, in whatsoever good work we do, we are serving you. Give us a diligent and watchful spirit, that we may seek in all things to know your will, and knowing it, gladly to perform it, to the honor and glory of your name; through Jesus Christ our Lord.

Gelasian Sacramentary

***Prayer of St. Benedict***

O gracious and Holy Father, give us wisdom to perceive you, diligence to seek you, patience to wait for you, eyes to behold you, a heart to meditate upon you, and a life to proclaim you, through the power of the Spirit of Jesus Christ our Lord.

***To Know You and to Love You***

Eternal God, who are the light of the minds that know you, the joy of the hearts that love you, and the strength of the wills that serve you, grant us so to know you that we may truly love you, and so to love you that we may fully serve you, whom to serve is perfect freedom, in Jesus Christ our Lord.

St. Augustine

***An Act of Surrender***

My God, I firmly believe that you are here and see me perfectly, and that you observe all my actions, all my thoughts, and the most secret movements of my heart. You permit me, a sinner who has so often offended you, to remain in your presence, and it is your goodness and bounty that command me to come to you. Give me grace, therefore, to pray as I should, and send your Holy Spirit upon me, to kindle in my heart the fire of your love.

Heavenly Father, I offer you the life and death of your Son, and with them my affections and resolutions, my thoughts, words, deeds, and sufferings this day and all my life, to honor your adorable majesty, to thank you for all your benefits, to satisfy for my sins, and to obtain the assistance of your grace, so that I may persevere to the end in doing your holy will and may love and enjoy you for ever in your glory.

God our Father, you know how weak I am. Do not leave me to myself, but take me under your protection, and give me grace to act upon my holy resolutions. Enlighten my understanding with a lively faith, raise up my will to a firm hope, and inflame it with an ardent charity. Strengthen my weakness, and cure the corruption of my heart. Grant that I may overcome the enemies of my soul and make good use of your grace, and if it be that I should die today, grant me the gift of final perseverance.

Heavenly Father, grant that by the guidance of the Holy Spirit, we may discern your holy will, and by the grace of the same Spirit we may also do it, gladly and with our whole hearts, for the glory of your Son Jesus Christ our Lord.

Grant us, O Lord, to pass this day in gladness and peace, without stumbling and without stain; that reaching the eventide victorious over all temptations, we may praise you, the eternal God, who are blessed and govern all things, world without end. Amen.

Mozarabic Liturgy

### *An Offering of the Day*

O God, our Father, we thank you for waking us to see the light of this new day. Grant that we may waste none of its hours, soil none of its moments, neglect none of its opportunities, fail in none of its duties. And bring us to the evening time undefeated by any temptation, at peace with ourselves and with you. This we ask for your love's sake.

William Barclay*

### *A Prayer for Light*

O God, Creator of light, at the rising of your sun this morning, let the greatest of all lights, your love, rise like the sun within our hearts.

Armenian Apostolic Church

### *A Prayer for Help*

O God, our Father, help us all through this day so to live that we may bring help to others, credit to ourselves and to the name we bear, and joy to those who love us and to you.

Cheerful when things go wrong;
Persevering when things are difficult;
Serene when things are irritating.
Enable us to be
Helpful to those in difficulties;
Kind to those in need;
Sympathetic to those whose hearts are sore and sad.
Grant that
Nothing may make us lose our tempers;
Nothing may take away our joy;

Nothing may ruffle our peace;
Nothing may make us bitter toward anyone.
So grant that through all this day all with whom we work, and all those whom we meet, may see in us the reflection of the Master, whose we are and whom we seek to serve. This we ask for your love's sake.

William Barclay

***Take This Day Into Your Keeping***

Dear Father, take this day's life into your own keeping. Control all my thoughts and feelings. Direct all my energies. Instruct my mind. Sustain my will. Take my hands and make them skillful to serve you. Take my feet and make them swift to do your bidding. Take my eyes and keep them fixed on your everlasting beauty. Take my mouth and make it eloquent in testimony of your love. Make this a day of obedience, a day of joy and peace. Make this day's work a little part of the work of the kingdom of my Lord Christ, in whose name my prayers are said.

John Baillie

***From Sunrise to Sunset***

As I begin this day,
become flesh again
in me, Father.
Let your timeless and everlasting love
live out this sunrise to sunset
within the possibilities
and the impossibilities
of my own, very human life.

Help me to become
Christ to my neighbor,
food to the hungry,
health to the sick,
friend to the lonely,
freedom to the enslaved,
in all my daily living.

J. Barrie Shepherd*

***Strengthen Our Weakness***

God, our Father, we are exceedingly frail and indisposed to every virtuous and gallant undertaking. Strengthen our weakness, we beseech you, that we may do valiantly in this spiritual war; help us against our own negligence and cowardice, and defend us from the treachery of our unfaithful hearts, for Jesus Christ's sake.

Thomas à Kempis

***Transform Our Minds***

Father in heaven, you have given us a mind to know you, a will to serve you, and a heart to love you. Be with us today in all that we do, so that your light may shine out in our lives.
We pray that we may be today what you created us to be and may praise your name in all that we do.
We pray for your Church:
May it be a true light to all nations.
May the Spirit of your Son Jesus
guide the words and actions of all Christians today.
We pray for all who are searching for truth:
bring them your light and your love.

Give us, Lord, a humble, quiet, peaceable, patient, tender, and charitable mind, and in all our thoughts, words, and deeds a taste of the Holy Spirit. Give us, Lord, a lively faith, a firm hope, a fervent charity, a love of you. Take from us all lukewarmness in meditation, dullness in prayer. Give us fervor and delight in thinking of you and your grace, your tender compassion toward us. The things that we pray for, good Lord, give us grace to labor for: through Jesus Christ our Lord.

St. Thomas More

***For the Presence of God***

Through every moment of this day: Be with me, Lord.
Through every day of all this week: Be with me, Lord.
Through every week of all this year: Be with me, Lord.
Through every year of all this life: Be with me, Lord.
So that when time is past,
By grace I may at last
Be with you, Lord.

***Be in Me***

God, be in my head and in my understanding;
God, be in my eyes and in my looking;
God, be in my mouth and in my speaking;
God, be in my heart and in my thinking;
God, be at my end and at my departing.

*The Book of Hours*

### *Aware of Your Presence*

Father, you are closer to me than my own breathing, as present and life-giving as my own heart. May each breath I take and each heartbeat I experience deepen my awareness of your presence.

Michael Buckley

### *God's Presence in My World*

Help me today to realize that you will be speaking to me through the events of the day, through people, through things, and through creation.
Give me ears, eyes, and heart to perceive you, however veiled your presence may be.
Give me insight to see through the exterior of things to the interior truth.
Give me your Spirit of discernment.
O Lord, you know how busy I must be this day.
If I forget you, do not forget me.

Jacob Astley

### *Searching for God*

O Lord my God,
teach my heart this day where and how to see you,
where and how to find you.
You have made me and remade me,
and you have bestowed on me
all the good things I possess,
and still I do not know you.
I have not yet done that

for which I was made.
Teach me to seek you,
for I cannot seek you
unless you teach me,
or find you
unless you show yourself to me.
Let me seek you in my desire,
Let me desire you in my seeking.
Let me find you by loving you,
Let me love you when I find you.

St. Anselm

***Trust in God's Providence***

My Lord God,
I have no idea where I am going.
I do not see the road ahead of me.
I cannot know for certain where it will end.
Nor do I really know myself,
and the fact that I think that I am following
your will does not mean that I am actually doing so.
But I believe that the desire to please you
does in fact please you.
And I hope I have that desire
in all that I am doing.
I hope that I will never do anything apart
from that desire.
And I know that if I do this,
you will lead me by the right road though I
may know nothing about it.

Therefore will I trust you always though I
  may seem lost and in the shadow of death.
I will not fear, for you are ever with me,
and you will never leave me to face my perils alone.

Thomas Merton

***For Service***

Teach us, good Lord,
to serve you as you deserve,
to give and not to count the cost,
to fight and not to heed the wounds,
to toil and not to seek for rest,
to labor and not to ask for any reward,
save that of knowing that we do your will;
through Jesus Christ our Lord.

St. Ignatius of Loyola

***In the Service of Others***

Make us worthy, Lord, to serve our fellow men throughout the world who live and die in poverty and hunger. Give them through our hands this day their daily bread, and by our understanding love, give peace and joy.

Mother Teresa of Calcutta

***In God's Service***

Lord God, whose we are and whom we serve,
help us to glorify you this day,
in all the thoughts of our hearts,
in all the words of our lips,
and in all the works of our hands,

as becomes those who are your servants,
through Jesus Christ our Lord.

*New Every Morning*

***Self-Offering***

Take, Lord, all my liberty. Receive my memory, my understanding, and my whole will. Whatever I have and possess, you have given me; to you I restore it wholly, and to your will I utterly surrender it for my direction. Give me the love of you only, with your grace, and I am rich enough; nor do I ask anything besides.

St. Ignatius of Loyola

***To God the Son***

Lord Jesus, grant this day to direct and sanctify, to rule and govern our hearts and bodies, so that all our thoughts, words, and deeds may be according to your Father's law, and thus may we be saved and protected through your mighty help.

***Morning Offering***

O Jesus, through the most pure heart of Mary, I offer you all the prayers, thoughts, works, and sufferings of this day, for all the intentions of your divine heart.

Grant, O Lord, that none may love thee less this day because of me;
that no word or act of mine may turn one soul from thee;
and ever daring, yet one other grace would I implore, that many souls this day, because of me,
may love thee more.

***Make Me an Instrument of Your Peace***

Lord, make me an instrument of your peace;
where there is hatred let me sow love,
where there is injury let me sow pardon,
where there is doubt let me sow faith,
where there is despair let me give hope,
where there is darkness let me give light,
where there is sadness let me give joy.
O divine master, grant that I may
not try to be comforted but to comfort,
not try to be understood but to understand,
not try to be loved but to love.
Because it is in giving that we receive,
it is in forgiving that we are forgiven,
and it is in dying that we are born to eternal life.

Ascribed to St. Francis of Assisi

***I Give Myself to You***

Lord Jesus,
I give you my hands to do your work.
I give you my feet to go your way.
I give you my eyes to see as you do.
I give you my tongue to speak your words.
I give you my mind that you may think in me.
I give you my spirit that you may pray in me.
Above all,
I give you my heart that you may love in me
your Father and all mankind.
I give you my whole self that you may grow in me,

so that it is you, Lord Jesus,
who live and work and pray in me.

*The Grail*

***To Your Care, Lord***

I hand over to your care, Lord,
my soul and body,
my mind and thoughts,
my prayers and my hopes,
my health and my work,
my life and my death,
my parents and my family,
my friends and my neighbors,
my country and all men.
Today and always.

Lancelot Andrewes

***According to Your Will***

O Lord Jesus Christ, who has created me and ordered my course and brought me here where I am; you know what you would make me; do with me according to your will, with mercy.

King Henry VI*

***A Blessing***

Lord Jesus,
Bless my memory this day, that it may ever recollect you.
Bless my understanding, that it may ever think of you.
Bless my will, that it may never seek or desire that which may

be displeasing to you.
Bless my body and all its actions.
Bless my heart with all its affections.
Bless me now and at the hour of my death.
Bless me in time and in eternity, and grant that your most sweet blessing may be to me a pledge of eternal happiness.
Bless my brethren, the faithful.
Bless my dear ones.
Bless everyone I love and everyone to whom I owe any gratitude, and bring me and them to rest in your Sacred Heart for ever.

***In Thanksgiving***

Thank you, Lord Jesus Christ,
for all the benefits you have given me,
for all the pains and insults you have borne for me.
O most merciful Redeemer, friend, and brother,
may I know you more clearly,
love you more dearly,
and follow you more nearly,
now and for ever.

St. Richard of Chichester

***For Divine Assistance***

May the strength of God guide me this day, and may his power preserve me.
May the wisdom of God instruct me; the eye of God watch over me;
the ear of God hear me; the word of God give sweetness to my speech;

the hand of God defend me; and may I follow the way of God.
Christ be with me, Christ before me,
Christ be after me, Christ within me,
Christ beneath me, Christ above me,
Christ at my right hand, Christ at my left,
Christ in the fort, Christ in the chariot,
Christ in the ship,
Christ in the heart of every man who thinks of me,
Christ in the mouth of every man who speaks to me.
Christ in every eye that sees me.
Christ in every ear that hears me.

St. Patrick's Breastplate

***Teach Me***

Guide me,
teach me,
strengthen me,
till I become like a person as you would
have me be,
pure and gentle, truthful and high-minded,
brave and able, courteous and generous,
dutiful and useful.

Charles Kingsley

***My Lord and My God***

My Lord and my God,
take me from all that keeps me from you.
My Lord and my God,
grant me all that leads me to you.

My Lord and my God,
take me from myself and give me completely to you.

Nicholas of Flue

***Safe Lodging and Holy Rest***

May the Lord support us all the day long, till the shades lengthen and the evening comes, and the busy world is hushed, and the fever of life is over, and our work is done. Then in his mercy, may he give us a safe lodging and a holy rest, and peace at the last. Father, we ask this through Jesus Christ our Lord.

St. John Henry Newman

***A Pure Heart***

Have mercy upon us.
Have mercy upon our efforts, that we
Before you, in love and in faith,
Righteousness and humility,
May follow you, with self-denial,
Steadfastness and courage,
And meet you in the silence.
Give us a pure heart that we may see you,
A humble heart that we may hear you,
A heart of love that we may serve you,
A heart of faith that we may love you.

Dag Hammarskjold*

***Watch Over Me***

O Jesus, watch over me always, especially today, or I shall betray you like Judas.

St. Philip Neri

### *Living Each Day to the Full*

Lord, let me live this day
as if it were my first day
or my last.
Let me bring to it
all the wonder and amazement of a newborn child;
the trust
that welcomes all I meet,
expects of them only the best,
and grants them the benefit
of every possible doubt;
But let me also bring
the wisdom and experience of the aged to this day;
the tenderness
that grows from years of care and gentle giving;
the hope that has been forged through all the fires of doubt.

J. Barrie Shepherd*

### *Resignation*

Lord Jesus, if you will that I be in darkness, may you be blessed: if you will that I be in light, may you equally be blessed. If you mercifully comfort me, may you be blessed, and if you will that I be afflicted, may you always equally be blessed. Keep me from all sin, and I shall fear neither death nor hell. So long as you do not cast me off for ever, nor blot me out of the Book of Life, no tribulation that befalls me will hurt me, because in all things I place my trust in your Sacred Heart.

*For Humility*

Lord, keep me
truly humble in whatever measure
of success this day may bring.
And grant, in all things,
whether failure or success,
that I might find you,
and finding you,
find all that I can ever ask
or hope for.

**At the Day's Close**

*To the Holy Trinity*

Most Holy Trinity, I commit my life, as I do this day, now drawing to a close, to your infinite mercy, trust, and love. For my lack of faith I ask mercy of the Father, who is swift to compassion and slow to anger; for my inability to trust your providence, I seek refuge in the humanity of the Son, who was obedient unto death; for my coldness in loving, I place myself in the warmth of the Holy Spirit, who alone makes our lives acceptable to you. May this night's repose refresh my body and soul, so that tomorrow's dawn may find me more ready to give glory to the Father, Son, and Holy Spirit.

Michael Buckley

*Keep Me*

Glory to thee, my God, this night
For all the blessings of the light;
Keep me, O keep me, King of Kings,

Beneath thine own almighty wings.
Forgive me, Lord, for thy dear Son,
The ill that I this day have done,
That with the world, myself, and thee,
I, ere I sleep, at peace may be.

Teach me to live, that I may dread
The grave as little as my bed;
Teach me to die, that so I may
Rise glorious at the awful day.
Praise God, from whom all blessings flow;
Praise him, all creatures here below;
Praise him above, ye heavenly host;
Praise Father, Son, and Holy Ghost.

Thomas Ken

***To God the Father***

Heavenly Father, at this hour that marks the end of the day, I come before you again in thankfulness to glorify your name. You have watched over me through the day, and now I seek your protection throughout the night. Send me calm rest to restore my body and soul, and strengthen my faith in you. When I arise in the morning, render me worthy to pray again to you and glorify your holy name.

Michael Buckley

***In Thanksgiving***

Almighty and eternal God, I believe all you have revealed to your holy Church, I hope in your infinite goodness and mercy, and I love you with all my heart. I thank you for all the favors that you have bestowed upon me this day; for my food and drink, my health, and all my powers of body and soul; for your holy lights and inspirations, your care and protection; and for all those other graces that I do not now recall or that I have not yet grown to value as I ought. I thank you for them all, heavenly Father, through Jesus Christ, your Son, our Lord.

***For Renewed Strength***

O God, with whom there is no darkness, but the night shines as the day: Keep and defend us and all your children, we beseech you, throughout the coming night. Renew our hearts with your forgiveness and our bodies with untroubled sleep, that we may wake to use more faithfully your gift of life, through Jesus Christ, our Lord. Amen.

***To the Lord of All***

Blessed be the Lord by day; blessed be the Lord by night; blessed be the Lord when we lie down; blessed be the Lord when we rise up. For in your hands are the souls of every living thing and the spirits of all human flesh. Into your hands I commend my spirit; you have redeemed me, O Lord, God of truth. Our Lord in heaven, assert the unity of your name, establish your kingdom continually, and reign over us forever and ever. Amen.

***Surrender to Grace***

Lord, may I be wakeful at sunrise to begin a new day for you; cheerful at sunset for having done my work for you;

thankful at moonrise and under starshine for the beauty of your universe. And may I add what little may be in me to add to your great world.

An Abbot of Greve

***Gratitude at Day's Close***

O Lord my God, thank you
  for bringing this day to a close;
Thank you for giving me rest
  in body and soul.
Your hand has been over me
  and has guarded and preserved me.
Forgive my lack of faith
  and any wrong that I have done today,
  and help me to forgive all who have wronged me.
Let me sleep in peace under your protection,
  and keep me from all the temptations of darkness.
Into your hands I commend my loved ones
  and all who dwell in this house;
I commend to you my body and soul.
O God, your holy name be praised.

Dietrich Bonhoeffer

***Gather Your Church***

We give thanks to you, our Father, for the life and knowledge you have imparted to us through Jesus your Son; glory be yours for ever. Even as...broken bread was scattered upon the hillside and then gathered up again, so let your Church be gathered together from the ends of the earth into your kingdom. For the kingdom, the power, and the glory are yours now and for ever.

The *Didache*

***Be Present***

Be present, O merciful God, and protect us through the silent hours of this night, that we who are wearied by the changes and chances of this fleeting world may repose upon your eternal changelessness, through the everlasting Christ our Lord.

Leonine Sacramentary

***A Prayer for Protection and Mercy***

O Lord our God, what sins I have this day committed in word, deed, or thought, forgive me, for you are gracious, and you love all men. Grant me peaceful and undisturbed sleep, send me your guardian angel to protect and guard me from every evil, for you are the guardian of our souls and bodies, and to you we ascribe glory, to the Father and the Son and the Holy Spirit, now and for ever and unto the ages of ages.

Russian Orthodox Prayer

***We Commend Our Lives***

Into your hands, O Lord and Father, we commend our souls and our bodies, our parents and our homes, friends and servants, neighbors and kindred, our benefactors and brethren departed, all your people faithfully believing, and all who need your pity and protection. Enlighten us with your holy grace, and suffer us never more to be separated from you, who are one God in Trinity, God everlasting. Amen.

St. Edmund of Abingdon

### *To God the Son*

Lord Jesus Christ, I offer you this night's repose in union with the eternal repose you have in the bosom of the Father and the temporal repose you had during your time on earth. I offer you every breath I shall draw this night and every motion of my heart as so many acts of love, praise, adoration, joy, thanksgiving, and homage that will be paid to you in heaven. I unite myself with your blessed mother, Mary, St. Joseph, and all the angels and saints, who will love and glorify you during this night and throughout all eternity.

*Loreto Manual*

### *Abide With Us*

Abide with us, Lord, for it is toward evening and the day is far spent; abide with us and with your whole Church. Abide with us in the evening of the day, in the evening of life, in the evening of the world. Abide with us and with all your faithful ones, O Lord, in time and eternity.

*Lutheran Manual of Prayer*

### *Watch Over Us*

Watch, dear Lord, with those who wake or watch or weep tonight, and give your angels charge over those who sleep. Tend your sick ones, O Lord Jesus Christ, rest your weary ones, bless your dying ones, soothe your suffering ones, shield your joyous ones, and all for your love's sake.

St. Augustine

***Your Loving Kindness***

Show your loving kindness tonight, O Lord, to all who stand in need of your help. Be with the weak to make them strong, and with the strong to make them gentle. Cheer the lonely with your company and the worried with your peace. Prosper your Church in the fulfillment of her mighty task, and grant your blessing to all who have toiled today in Christ's name.

John Baillie

***To the Holy Spirit***

Holy Spirit, as the day ends and the dawn of salvation draws ever closer, we thank you for your presence, which throughout the day sanctified our lives and took our fleeting moments into the bosom of the Father. We ask pardon for those lapses when, through sloth and willfulness, we forgot to live by your Spirit, without which nothing is acceptable to the Father. We ask you this night for a quiet rest, and at the end your eternal peace, which surpasses all understanding.

Michael Buckley

***Surrender to the Holy Spirit***

Holy Spirit, I thank you for being with me this day, for all the happiness your will has brought, and for all the toil and hardships I have had to accept. Forgive me for the times when I have forgotten you amid the cares of life. Forgive me also if I have not accepted any suffering in the same spirit as Christ my Lord. Help me to rest in peace this night, that I may wake truly refreshed and willing to spend a new day in your service. Guard me this night, as the good shepherd guards his flock. Grant that, in your mercy and love, when I close my eyes on this world for the last time, I may wake in the joy of your presence to a new, everlasting day.

Harold Winstone

***The Quiet Voice of the Spirit***

Holy Spirit, I thank you for the quiet moments of this busy day when you spoke to me of your abiding love. Teach me now as I lie down to rest how to listen to you when you speak in the silence of the night, in the silence of my heart. Teach me waking or sleeping how to watch and how to listen for your still, small voice, which gives meaning and direction to every moment of my life.

Michael Buckley

***For the House and Family***

Visit, we beseech you, O Lord, this house and family, and drive far from it all the snares of the enemy; let your holy angels dwell herein, who will keep us in peace, and let your blessing be always upon us, through our Lord Jesus Christ.

***For the Less Fortunate***

O God, our Father, we ask you to bless those for whom there will be no sleep tonight; those who must work throughout the night to maintain the public services; doctors who must wake to usher new life into the world, to close the eyes of those for whom this life is passing away, to ease the sufferer's pain;

nurses and all who watch by the bedside of those who are ill; those who this night will not sleep because of the pain of their body or the distress of their mind; those in misfortune, who will lie down in hunger and in cold; those who are far from home and far from friends, and who are lonely as the shadows fall. Grant that in our own happiness and comfort we may never forget the sorrow and the pain, the loneliness and the need of others in the slow, dark hours. This we ask for your love's sake.

William Barclay

***General Blessing***

May the Lord bless us, and preserve us from all evil, and bring us to life everlasting; and may the souls of the faithful, through the mercy of God, rest in peace.

*Manual of Our Lady*

***For a Happy Death***

Jesus, Mary, and Joseph, I give you my heart and my soul.
Jesus, Mary, and Joseph, assist me in my last agony.
Jesus, Mary, and Joseph, may I breathe forth my soul in peace with you.

***Nunc Dimittis***

At last, all powerful master, you give leave to your servant to go in peace, according to your promise. For my eyes have seen your salvation, which you have prepared for all nations, the light to enlighten the Gentiles and give glory to Israel, your people. Give praise to the Father almighty, to his Son, Jesus

Christ, the Lord, to the Spirit, who dwells in our hearts, both now and forever. Amen.

See Luke 2:29–32

***An Act of Faith, Hope, and Love at the End of the Day***

O my God, I accept my death as a homage and adoration that I owe to your divine majesty, and as a punishment justly due my sins, in union with the death of my dear Redeemer and as the only means of coming to you, my beginning and last end. I firmly believe all the sacred truths that the Catholic Church believes and teaches, because you have revealed them. And by the assistance of your holy grace, I am resolved to live and die in the communion of your Church.

Relying upon your goodness, power, and promises, I hope to obtain pardon of my sins and life everlasting through the merits of your Son, Jesus Christ, my only Redeemer, and by the intercession of his blessed mother and all the saints.

I love you with all my heart and soul, and I desire to love you as the blessed do in heaven. I adore all the designs of your divine providence, resigning myself entirely to your will.

I also love my neighbor for your sake, as I love myself; I forgive all who have injured me, and I ask pardon of all whom I have injured.

I renounce the devil, with all his works; the world, with all its empty show; the flesh, with all its temptations.

I desire to be dissolved and to be with Christ. Father, into your hands I commend my spirit.

**Lord Jesus, receive my soul.**

May the Blessed Virgin Mary, St. Joseph, and all the saints pray for us to our Lord, that we may be preserved this night from sin and all evils.

**Amen.**

Blessed St. Michael, defend us in the day of battle, that we may not be lost at the dreadful judgment.

**Amen.**

O my good angel, whom God, by his divine mercy, has appointed to be my guardian, enlighten and protect me, direct and govern me this night.

**Amen.**

May the almighty and merciful Lord give us pardon, absolution, and remission of our sins.

**Amen.**

Grant, O Lord, this night,

**To keep us without sin.**

Have mercy on us, O Lord.

**Have mercy on us.**

Let your mercy, O Lord, be upon us,

**As we have hoped in you.**

O Lord, hear my prayer,

**And let my cry come to you.**

Let us pray:
Visit, we beseech you, O Lord, this house and family, and drive far from it all the snares of the enemy; let your holy angels dwell herein, who may keep us in peace, and let your blessing be always upon us.
Through Christ our Lord.
**Amen.**

## FAMILY PRAYER

*The Christian family is the Church in its smallest and most powerful form. When the family gathers together to pray, Christ is in their midst in a special way. He blesses the father, mother, and children in their unique relationship with one another. Through sharing in prayer the family grows together in Christ.*

### *For the Family: Parents and Children*

Heavenly Father, bless us all this day. In our lives at work, at school, and at home, help us always to do your holy will and to know that in doing it we are pleasing to you and fulfilling your plan for our salvation.

Michael Buckley

### *For Appreciation of Each Other*

We thank you, Father, for the gift of Jesus your Son, who came to our earth and lived in a simple home. We have a greater appreciation of the value and dignity of the human family because he loved and was loved within its shelter. Bless us this day; may we grow in love for each other in our family and so give thanks to you who are the maker of all human families and our abiding peace.

Michael Buckley

### *To the Holy Spirit*

Holy Spirit, be with us throughout this day.
Strengthen us in our work, enlighten us in our study, make us constantly aware of each other and of you, so that we will live every moment of this day as you would have us do.

Michael Buckley

***For the Family***

Father, we pray for the family of all mankind, that they may acknowledge you as their Creator and provider; for the family of our nation, that we may live in peace and encourage other nations to do likewise; for the families of this neighborhood, with whom you have chosen us to share your presence. Finally, for our own family, that your peace may descend upon us, so that from our inner awareness of your presence we may witness your love for the whole human family.

Michael Buckley

***In Gratitude***

Thank you, Father, for having created us and given us to each other in the human family.

Thank you for being with us in all our joys and sorrows, for your comfort in our sadness, for your companionship in our loneliness.

Thank you for yesterday, today, tomorrow, and the whole of our lives.

Thank you for friends, for health, and for grace.

May we live this and every day conscious of all that has been given to us.

Michael Buckley

***For Harmony***

Lord Jesus Christ, be with us as a family so that we may always have a great love for your Sacred Heart. Make us gentle, courteous, and loving in our dealings with each other; take from us all misunderstanding, so that no angry or bitter word may cross our lips, and grant that we always treat each other as you treated those with whom you shared your human family.

Michael Buckley

***Protection for the Family***

Lord Jesus Christ,
I praise and thank you for my parents and
my brothers and sisters,
whom you have given me to cherish.
Surround them with your tender, loving care,
and teach them to love and serve one another
in true affection
and to look to you in all their needs.
I place them all in your care,
knowing that your love for them is greater than my own.
Keep us close to one another in this life,
and conduct us at the last to our true
and heavenly home.
Blessed be God for ever. Amen.

***For True Christian Homes***

Lord Jesus, who grew up in an earthly home obedient to earthly parents, bless all the homes in this parish. May the parents impart to their children the knowledge of you and your love, and may the children love, obey, and succor their parents; and bring us all to the joy of your heavenly home, for your great name's sake.

*A Parent's Prayer*

Heavenly Father, from whom all parenthood comes, teach us so to understand our children that they may grow in your wisdom and love according to your holy will. Fill us with sensitive respect for the great gift of human life that you have committed to our care, help us to listen with patience to their worries and problems, and give us the tolerance to allow them to develop, as individuals, as your Son did under the loving guidance of Mary and Joseph.

Michael Buckley

***For Parents***

Father, bless the parents of this home. Help them in all their endeavors, sustain them in their trials, give them wisdom and strength to meet their responsibilities, and may they in their love for each other and for us find true joy, peace, and fulfillment.

*A Father's Prayer*

Father, give me, like Joseph, a conscience sensitive to your holy will, so that I may accept in my family those things that I do not understand. May I, like him, put the good of my wife and children above my own self-interest and thus bring to fulfillment the mysterious workings of your providence for our family.

Michael Buckley

### *A Mother's Prayer*

Father, lover of life and of the human family, who cooperated with me in the birth of my children, be with me now and help me in my task of raising them as children of your kingdom. May they give you constant praise and adoration and be to me a never-ending source of gratitude and thanksgiving.

Michael Buckley

### *For Children*

Lord Jesus, who loved the little ones, bless the children of this family; guide and protect them through their growing years and throughout their lives. Be to them a true shepherd, and suffer them not to fall away from your love and service. May they always listen to your voice, because they know you as their Lord and Savior.

Michael Buckley

### *An Expectant Mother's Prayer*

Father, may the little unborn one who lies close to my heart grow strong day by day until the time of his or her birth. At the hour of delivery, may I not be afraid of the pains I may have to suffer but rejoice at the birth of another person destined to share with me in the human family in this world and the world to come.

### *For Growth in Family Love*

Lord, a healthy sexual relationship is so important in marriage, that we want to thank you for ours. The priest who prepared us for marriage told us that the sacraments are signs of your loving presence. Please help us not to forget that the sign of our sacrament, the sexual expression of our love, makes you present in our home. Please continue to enrich our lives and our family with your loving presence.

Tony Castle

***For All Who Are Dear to Us***

O God, by the grace of the Holy Spirit, you have filled the hearts of your faithful Christians with gifts of love. Grant health of mind and body to your servants, the men and women for whom we beseech your kindness: may they love you with all their strength and do your will with all their heart.

***Grace Before Meals***

Bless us, O Lord, and these your gifts, which we are about to receive from your bounty. Through Christ our Lord. Amen.

***Grace After Meals***

We give you thanks, almighty God, for all your benefits (gifts), who lives and reigns, for ever and ever. Amen.

***A Selection of Graces***

Lord Jesus, be our holy guest,
Our morning prayer,
Our evening rest,
And with this daily food impart
Thy love and grace to every heart.

A Grace Used by President Eisenhower

Come, Lord Jesus, be our guest,
and bless what thou hast given us.

Old German Grace

Lord Jesus, who when you were on earth celebrated a meal with joy, be with us now, and fill us with your spirit as we share food and fellowship together.

Michael Buckley

We thank you, Lord, not only for this food but for all your many blessings that you shower upon us.
Bless, O Lord, this food to our use and ourselves to your service, through Jesus Christ our Lord.
May the food that we bless in your name, O Lord, give us the strength to serve you, through Jesus Christ our Lord.

*This doxology is often sung as a blessing:*
Praise God from whom all blessings flow,
Praise him, all creatures here below,
Praise him above, angelic host,
Praise Father, Son, and Holy Ghost.

Thomas Ken

Blessed be thou, Lord God of the universe,
who bringest forth bread from the earth
and makest glad the heart of men.

Ancient Hebrew Prayer

Be present at our table, Lord,
Be here and everywhere adored:
These creatures bless, and grant that we
May feast in paradise with thee.

John Cennick

Heavenly Father, bless this food, bless those who have prepared it, and give food to those who at this time go hungry in our world.

Michael Buckley

## PRAYING CONTINUALLY

*The Spirit of the risen Christ is always at work in us. Through him we praise, honor, and adore God our loving Father, so that our minds and hearts are at rest in him. Our prayer, like our lives, is through Jesus Christ our Lord. His name is never far from our lips, so that our lives are a perpetual offering of prayer to the Father.*

### *Divine Mercy Chaplet*

Pray using your rosary.

1. Begin with the Sign of the Cross, one Our Father, one Hail Mary and The Apostles' Creed.
2. Then on the Our Father beads say the following:

Eternal Father, I offer You the Body and Blood, Soul and Divinity of Your dearly beloved Son, Our Lord Jesus Christ, in atonement for our sins and those of the whole world.

3. On the ten Hail Mary beads say the following:

For the sake of his sorrowful Passion, have mercy on us and on the whole world.

*(Repeat steps 2 and 3 for all five decades).*

4. Conclude with *(three times)*:

Holy God, Holy Mighty One, Holy Immortal One, have mercy on us and on the whole world.

### *The Jesus Prayer*

*The power of the invocation lies in the holy name itself, "Jesus." The name is the prayer. Phrases from the litany of the holy name may prove a source of great help in deepening our awareness of the presence and power of God's Son and our Savior.*

Lord Jesus Christ,
Son of the living God,
Have mercy on me, a sinner.

***The Litany of the Most Holy Name of Jesus***

Lord, have mercy on us.
    Lord, have mercy on us.
Christ, have mercy on us.
    Christ, have mercy on us.
Lord, have mercy on us.
    Lord, have mercy on us.
Jesus, hear us.
    Jesus, graciously hear us.
God the Father of heaven,
    have mercy on us.
God the Son, Redeemer of the world,
    have mercy on us.
God the Holy Spirit,
    have mercy on us.
Holy Trinity, one God,
    have mercy on us.
Jesus, Son of the living God,
    have mercy on us.
Jesus, splendor of the Father
    have mercy on us.

Jesus, brightness of eternal light,
have mercy on us.
Jesus, King of Glory,
have mercy on us.
Jesus, Son of Justice,
have mercy on us.
Jesus, Son of the Virgin Mary,
have mercy on us.
Jesus most amiable,
have mercy on us.
Jesus most admirable,
have mercy on us.
Jesus, mighty God,
have mercy on us.
Jesus, father of the world to come,
have mercy on us.
Jesus, angel of great counsel,
have mercy on us.
Jesus most powerful,
have mercy on us.
Jesus most patient,
have mercy on us.
Jesus most obedient,
have mercy on us.
Jesus, meek and humble of heart,
have mercy on us.
Jesus, lover of purity,
have mercy on us.

Jesus, lover of us,
have mercy on us.
Jesus, Author of life,
have mercy on us.
Jesus, perfection of all virtues,
have mercy on us.
Jesus, zealous lover of souls,
have mercy on us.
Jesus, our refuge,
have mercy on us.
Jesus, father of the poor,
have mercy on us.
Jesus, treasure of the faithful
have mercy on us.
Jesus, Good Shepherd,
have mercy on us.
Jesus, true light,
have mercy on us.
Jesus, eternal wisdom,
have mercy on us.
Jesus, infinite goodness,
have mercy on us.
Jesus, our way and our life,
have mercy on us.
Jesus, joy of angels,
have mercy on us.
Jesus, King of patriarchs,
have mercy on us.

Jesus, Master of the apostles,
have mercy on us.
Jesus, teacher of the evangelists,
have mercy on us.
Jesus, strength of martyrs,
have mercy on us.
Jesus, light of confessors,
have mercy on us.
Jesus, purity of virgins,
have mercy on us.
Jesus, crown of all saints,
have mercy on us.
Be merciful unto us,
Jesus, spare us.
Be merciful unto us,
Jesus, spare us.
From all evil,
Jesus, deliver us.
From all sin,
Jesus, deliver us.
From your wrath,
Jesus, deliver us.
From the snares of the devil,
Jesus, deliver us.
From everlasting death,
Jesus, deliver us.
From our failure to follow your inspiration,
Jesus, deliver us.

Through the mystery of your holy incarnation,
Jesus, deliver us.
Through your nativity,
Jesus, deliver us.
Through your infancy,
Jesus, deliver us.
Through your most divine life,
Jesus, deliver us.
Through your labors,
Jesus, deliver us.
Through your agony and passion,
Jesus, deliver us.
Through your cross and abandonment,
Jesus, deliver us.
Through your death and burial,
Jesus, deliver us.
Through your resurrection,
Jesus, deliver us.
Through your ascension,
Jesus, deliver us.
Through your reign in heaven,
Jesus, deliver us.
Through your joys,
Jesus, deliver us.
Through your glory,
Jesus, deliver us.
Lamb of God, you take away the sins of the world,
Spare us, O Jesus.

Lamb of God, you take away the sins of the world.
Graciously hear us, O Jesus.
Lamb of God, you take away the sins of the world.
Jesus, graciously hear us.

Let us pray:
Lord Jesus Christ, who has said: Ask and you shall receive; seek, and you shall find; knock, and it shall be opened unto you, mercifully listen to our prayers and grant us the gift of your divine mercy, that we may ever love you with our whole heart and never cease from praising and glorifying your holy name. Give us, O Lord, a perpetual love of your holy name; for you never cease to be with those whom you establish in your love. Who lives and reigns world without end. Amen.

***Aspirations or Short Prayers***
To you be praise,
To you be glory,
To you be thanksgiving
through endless ages, O blessed Trinity.
Holy Trinity, one God, have mercy on us.
Holy, holy, holy, Lord God of hosts:
the heavens and the earth are full of your glory.
To the King of ages, immortal and invisible,
to God alone be honor and glory
for ever and ever.
Blessing and glory and wisdom and thanksgiving,
honor, might, and power be unto our God for
ever and ever.

May the most just, most high, and most lovable will
of God be done in all things, be praised and worshipped
forever.
My God and my all.
My God, make us to be of one mind in the truth
and of one heart in charity.
My God, I love you.
Lord, I am my own enemy when I see my peace apart from
you.
Keep me as the apple of the eye;
hide me in the shadow of your wings.

Psalm 17:8

Teach me, O Lord, to do your will, for you are my
God.
Into your hand I commit my spirit.

Psalm 31:5

O my soul, I love the Lord that loves you from eternity.
...
O LORD, make haste to help me!
...
I am poor and needy;
hasten to me, O God!

Psalm 70:1, 5

From all dangers deliver us, O Lord.
O Lord, grant this day
to keep us without sin.
From all sin deliver us, O Lord.

Eternal Father, I offer you the precious blood of Jesus in satisfaction for my sins and for the needs of the Church.
Jesus, my God, I love you above all things.
O Jesus, with all my heart I cling to you.
Jesus, for love of you, with you and for you.
Praised be Jesus Christ
now and forever.
My Jesus, mercy.
My sweetest Jesus, be not my judge but my Savior.
O Jesus, be to me Jesus, and save me.
O Christ Jesus, my helper and my Redeemer.
Deliver me, Lord Jesus Christ, from all my iniquities and from every evil. Make me ever hold fast to your commandments, and never allow me to be separated from you.
We adore you, O Christ, and we bless you;
because by your holy cross you have redeemed the world.
Sacred Heart of Jesus, protect our families.
Heart of Jesus, burning with love for us,
inflame our hearts with love for you.
Sweet Heart of Jesus,
grant that I may love you more.
Heart of Jesus, I place all my trust in you.
Jesus, meek and humble of heart,
make my heart like unto yours.
O Heart of love, I put all my trust in you;
for I fear all things from my own weakness,
but I hope for all things from your goodness.

Most Sacred Heart of Jesus,
have mercy on us.

O sweetest Heart of Jesus, I implore
that I may ever love you more and more.

May the Sacred Heart of Jesus be everywhere loved.

Sacred Heart of Jesus, I believe in your love for me.

All for you, most Sacred Heart of Jesus, all for you.

Sweet Heart of Jesus, be my love.

Sacred Heart of Jesus, let me love you and make you loved.

May the most holy and most divine Sacrament be every moment praised and adored.

Blessed be the holy and Immaculate Conception of the most Blessed Virgin Mary, Mother of God.

Mary, Mother of God and Mother of Mercy, pray for me and for the departed.

O Mary, conceived without sin, pray for us who have recourse to you.

Pray for us, O holy Mother of God,
that we may be made worthy of the promises of Christ.

O Mary, make me live in God, with God, and for God.

Draw me after you, Holy Mother.

O Mary, may your children persevere in loving you.

*No situation is outside the light of the Resurrection, the power of the Holy Spirit, or God the Father's love. Every aspect of our lives is under this powerful influence. When we pray, whether it be for the needs of the world or our own spiritual growth, then God is there to meet our every desire. If we ask for bread, he will not give us a stone.*

**For the Church**

***Early Christian Prayer***

Think of your Church, O Lord. Free it from all evil, and make it perfect in your love. Make your people holy, and lead them to the kingdom you have prepared for them. For yours is the power and the glory for all eternity.

***Prayer for Perseverance***

Almighty and everlasting God, who has revealed your glory in Christ among the nations: Preserve the works of your mercy, that your Church, which is spread throughout the world, may persevere with steadfast faith and love in the confession of your name, through Jesus Christ our Lord.

Gelasian Sacramentary

***His Divine Mission***

God, your Son left his Church as a memorial of his presence and as a witness of his divine mission. May all Christians grow in the exercise of faith, hope, and love, that her life will be so renewed that she, who is the light of the world, may shine brightly before everyone.

## For the Body of Christ

### *For the Local Church or Parish*

O God, the Creator, redeemer, and sanctifier of all who believe and trust in you, bless the Church in this place in its work for the furtherance of your kingdom on earth. Strengthen the faith and commitment of its members, deepen the bonds of community, and grant to all a spirit of sharing, generosity, and self-sacrifice.

Michael Buckley

### *For the Intercession of the Saints*

Keep us safe, Lord, from every danger that threatens mind or body. In your goodness give peace and security, asked for us by the prayers of the blessed and glorious ever-virgin Mary, Mother of God, of blessed Joseph, of your blessed apostles Peter and Paul, of blessed N. and of all the saints; so that all hostility and falsehood may be brought to nothing, and your Church may serve you in untroubled freedom.

### *For the Persecuted Church*

Mercifully hear the prayers of your Church, Lord, that all hostility and falsehood may be brought to nothing, and that she may serve you in untroubled freedom.

### *For the Pope*

O almighty and eternal God, have mercy on your servant our pope, and direct him into the way of everlasting salvation. May he desire by your grace those things that are agreeable to you and perform them with all his strength. Through Christ our Lord. Amen.

O God, shepherd and ruler of all the faithful, look favorably on your servant N. whom you have made chief pastor of your Church. May his words and example profit those over whom he is placed, so that he and his flock may together attain everlasting life.

***For Priests***

Lord Jesus, bless all priests, and give them grace to do your great work on earth. Keep them, Lord, close to your heart and under the shadow of your protection. Bless their labors for you, and grant that their harvest of souls may be a source of joy and consolation to them during life and may merit an everlasting reward for them in death, that having led many souls to you they may see you face-to-face.

***For Vocations***

Lord Jesus Christ, shepherd of souls, who called the apostles to be fishers of men, raise up new apostles in your holy Church. Teach them that to serve you is to reign, to possess you is to possess all things. Kindle in the young hearts of our sons and daughters the fire of zeal for souls. Make them eager to spread your kingdom upon earth. Grant them courage to follow you, who are the way, the truth, and the life, who lives and reigns for ever and ever. Amen.

*A Simple Prayer Book*

***For Christian Discipleship***

Lord our God, you have given your Son to the world, and in his Church he nourishes his faithful with the gospel and the sacraments. We ask you that Christians everywhere may find strength to tread his path; and that they be for each other and with each other, so that the power of your grace may shine through their lives. Through Christ our Lord.

***For Christian Unity***

That they may all be one, even as you, Father, are in me, and I in you…so that the world may believe that you have sent me.

John 17:21

Let us pray:
O God of Peace, who through your Son Jesus Christ did proclaim one faith for the salvation of mankind, send your grace and blessing on all Christians who are striving to draw nearer to you and to each other. Give us boldness to seek only your glory and the advancement of your kingdom. Unite us all in you, Father, who with your Son and the Holy Spirit are one God, for ever and ever.

O God, you bring back to the right way those who have gone astray, you gather the scattered, and you keep together those you have gathered. Mercifully fill Christian people with the grace of your own oneness, that they may reject all division and, being one in communion with the true shepherd of your Church, be able to serve you as you should be served.

***For the Missions***

You desire, O God, that all men should come to know truth and all be saved. Send then, we pray, workers into your harvest field, and give them power boldly to proclaim your word. Thus may your gospel be received and honored throughout the world, and every people know you, the one true God, and your Son whom you have sent, our Lord Jesus Christ.

***For the Spread of the Gospel***

Almighty God, from whom all thoughts of truth and peace proceed, kindle, we pray, in the hearts of all men the true love of peace, and guide with your pure and peaceable wisdom those who take counsel for the nations of the earth; that in tranquility your kingdom may go forward, till the earth is filled with the knowledge of your love; through Jesus Christ our Lord. Amen.

Lord, your love and salvation were meant for everyone, and Christians are your missionaries. Because you have made Christians one in Christ, so those who believe and are baptized have brothers and sisters all over the world—in Africa, Asia, America, Australia, and Europe. Grant that this life of Christ may grow stronger, drawing them ever closer together in love and unity and helping them to become more zealous for the spread of the gospel.

## For the World

***For the Enlightenment of the Nations***

Almighty God, who led the wise men by the light of a star to your infant Son, to worship in him the glory of the Word made flesh: guide by your truth the nations of the earth that, imitating the wise men, the whole world may find your Son.

*A Christian's Prayer Book*

### *For a Correct Attitude Toward the World*

O Lord, grant that we may not be conformed to the world but may love it and serve it. Grant that we may never shrink from being instruments of your peace because of the judgment of the world. Grant that we may love you without fear of the world; grant that we may never believe that the inexpressible majesty of yourself may be found in any power of this earth. May we firstly love you and our neighbors as ourselves. May we remember the poor and the prisoner, and the sick and the lonely, and the young searchers, and the tramps and vagabonds, and the lost and lonely, as we remember Christ, who is in them all.

Alan Paton

### *For Patriotism*

Heavenly Father, purify in all the people of this land their love for the nation, according to the mind of your Son Jesus Christ, who knew what was good for the peace of his land and people. May everyone strive by word and action to foster peace among people of all social classes and creeds, so that, living in harmony and justice, they may be a Christian light to other nations, such as your Son would have them be.

Michael Buckley

### *For the Fallen in Battle*

Heavenly Father, we remember before you, with gratitude, those who gave their lives for the cause of our nation. Because you have taken them to yourself, they shall not grow old as we that are left grow old. Age shall not weary them, nor the years condemn. Grant that their sacrifice may bear fruit in the Christian quality of our lives and all those who share with them a common fatherland.

Laurence Binyon*

***For Peace and Justice***

Almighty and eternal God, may your grace enkindle in all of us a love for the many unfortunate people whom poverty and misery reduce to a condition of life unworthy of human beings. Arouse in the hearts of those who call you Father a hunger and thirst for justice and peace and for fraternal charity in deeds and in truth. Grant, O Lord, peace in our days, peace to souls, peace to families, peace to our country, and peace among nations.

Pope Pius XII

***For Social Justice and Peace***

Jesus, Son of God, friend of all social classes, grant that the rich may so evaluate their wealth that they may generously follow the simplicity of your dedicated life and so help the poor to lead a life worthy of their human dignity. Grant that all may see themselves as your brothers and sisters, you who became poor for our sake.

Michael Buckley

***For Immigrants***

Father, conscious that your Son, while still an infant, made his home in a foreign land, we pray for all those from other countries who now live among us. May their customs and culture be appreciated, and may they be offered true Christian friendship and understanding as a token of gratitude for that welcome that was once offered to your only Son.

Michael Buckley

***Prayer to End Abortion***

Lord God, I thank you today for the gift of my life,
And for the lives of all my brothers and sisters.
I know there is nothing that destroys more life than abortion,
Yet I rejoice that you have conquered death
By the Resurrection of Your Son.
I am ready to do my part in ending abortion.
Today I commit myself
Never to be silent,
Never to be passive,
Never to be forgetful of the unborn.
I commit myself to be active in the pro-life movement,
And never to stop defending life
Until all my brothers and sisters are protected,
And our nation once again becomes
A nation with liberty and justice
Not just for some, but for all.
Through Christ our Lord. Amen!

Fr. Frank Pavone, Priests for Life

***Prayer to Mary, Mother of the Life Within***

O Mary, Mother of the Life Within,
all life we entrust to you;
The life of every expectant mother
and the child within her womb:

The life of every human body,
the life of every human soul;
The life of every newborn child
and the life of all grown old.
You held the Lord to your own heart
and drew Him so close in.
So draw us now in all our needs,
O Mother of the Life Within.
Amen.

Priests for Life

***For Industrial Peace***

Father, your love taught us that we are members of one family; grant that all employers and employees, conscious of their mutual rights and obligations, may avoid bitterness and distrust in industrial disputes and work together for the good of our nation and people.

Michael Buckley

***General Intercession for Peace***

In peace, let us beseech the Lord
for the peace that is from above
and the salvation of our souls;
for the peace of the whole world
and of the holy churches of God
and of all men.
For our homes, that they may be holy,
and for all our pastors, teachers, and governors;
for our city (township, village) and country

and all who dwell therein;
for all that travel by land, by air, by water;
for the sick and all who need your pity and protection.
On all have mercy, and preserve all, O God, by your grace:
for to you, O Lord, is due glory, honor, and worship, world without end.

Liturgy of St. John Chrysostom

**For Workers**

***For Good Use of Time***

Lord, time is your gift to me, and through it, you who are eternal, enter my life and world. Guide, inspire, and help me to fill every moment of every hour, full to the brim with your presence, so that it may overflow to others round me and quench their thirst for a true meaning to life.

Michael Buckley

Lord, help me use time well, especially when I am waiting for my next task, just as you waited in Nazareth before beginning your public life and during that time grew daily in age and wisdom before God and men.

Michael Buckley

Lord, give me the grace to work to bring about the things that I pray for.

St. Thomas More

Lord, give me faith to believe that all work, however humble, is sanctified by your presence when we offer it to the Father, just as you offered your lowly work as a carpenter in Nazareth to the glory of his name.

Michael Buckley

As tools come to be sharpened by the blacksmith, so may we come, O Lord. As sharpened tools go back with their owner, so may we go back to our everyday life and work, to be used by thee, O Lord.

Prayer of Zande Christians

***For Writers, Artists, and Those in Media***

Almighty God, who has proclaimed your eternal truth by the voice of the prophets and evangelists: direct and bless, we ask you, those who, in this our generation, speak where many listen and write what many read; that they may do their part in making the heart of the people wise, its mind sound, and its will righteous; to the honor of Jesus Christ our Lord.

*The Boys' Prayer Book*

***For Students***

Grant, Lord, to all students, to love and know that which is worth loving and knowing, to praise that which pleases you most, to esteem that which is most precious to you, and to dislike whatsoever is evil in your eyes.

Thomas à Kempis

***For the Unemployed***

Heavenly Father, who wills that every individual should belong to the human community, look with compassion on those who suffer distress through lack of work; take from them the feeling of rejection. Grant that they be set free from want and insecurity, and may they soon find employment, as did those in the gospel story who were called at the eleventh hour to labor in the vineyard, through Jesus Christ, our Lord. Amen.

Michael Buckley

### *For Work*

God our Father,
through and by the work of our hands,
your mighty work of creation continues.
Hear the prayers of your people,
and give all who seek employment
the opportunity to enhance their human dignity
and draw closer to one another
in mutual interdependence.

Tony Castle

## For the Suffering, Sick, and Dying

### *For the Sick*

Almighty and ever-living God, physician who brings eternal healing to those who believe, hear us as we ask your compassionate help for your servant N. who is sick. Give him (her) back good health, and enable him (her) to return thanks to you in the assembly of the faithful.

### *For a Happy Death*

Almighty and merciful God, mankind receives from you the means of salvation and the grace to attain everlasting life. Look kindly on all your servants, and fortify the souls you have created, so that when the hour of departure comes, they may be free from sin and fit to be brought by the holy angels to you in your glory.

***For Those Suffering From an Incurable Disease***

Father, lover of life, we pray for those suffering from disease for which, at present, there is no known cure; give them confidence in your love and never-failing support and a strong faith in the Resurrection. Grant wisdom and perseverance to all working to discover the causes of the disease, so that they see in their labors the ministry of your Son, who himself showed forth his divine power by healing those who came to him.

George Appleton

***For Those Who Mourn***

Lord Jesus Christ, you wept over the death of Lazarus and said, "Blessed are those who mourn" (Matthew 5:5). Visit with your compassion, we beseech you, the homes and hearts of those who mourn the loss of their loved one. May their hope in the Resurrection sustain them in this hour of trial.

***For the Distressed***

God, whose mercy and compassion never fail, look kindly upon the sufferings of all mankind: the needs of the homeless; the anxieties of prisoners; the pains of the sick and the injured; the sorrows of the bereaved; the helplessness of the aged and weak. Comfort and strengthen them for the sake of your Son, our Savior Jesus Christ.

St. Anselm

### *For the Homeless*

Have mercy, O Lord our God, on those whom war or oppression or famine has robbed of homes and friends, and aid all those who try to help them. We commend also into your care those whose homes are broken by conflict and lack of love; grant that where the love of man has failed, the divine compassion may heal; through Jesus Christ our Lord.

### *For the Aged*

Lord Jesus Christ, who heard the prayers of your two disciples at Emmaus and stayed with them at eventide, stay, we pray you, with all your people in the evening of their life. Make yourself known to them, and let your light shine upon their path; and whenever they shall pass through the valley of the shadow of death, be with them to the end.

George Appleton

## For Travelers

### *For Those on a Journey or Pilgrimage*

Hear our prayers, Lord, and give your servants a safe and happy journey; and may your help be with them in all the changes and chances of their way through this life.

### *For Those at Sea*

You, O God, brought our spiritual forefathers through the Red Sea, leading them by deep waters while they sang praises to your name. We beg you to watch over your servants who are aboard ship, give them a good passage, and bring them safely to harbor.

### *For Those Who Travel by Air*

O God, protector of those who trust in your power, send a good angel from heaven to go with travelers through the air, that they may be watched over in their journey and brought safely to their destination.

O Almighty God, who makest the clouds thy chariots, and walkest upon the wings of the wind: we beseech thee for all who travel by air to their several duties and destinations: that thy presence may ever be with them, to pilot, to speed, and to protect, through Jesus Christ our Lord.

Eric Milner-White

### *For Motorists*

Almighty God, ever active and ever at rest, give us a mind so set at peace with you that we may use our vehicles with a true spirit of courtesy and respect for others, so that avoiding all unnecessary tension, anxiety, and desire for speed, we may protect others and ourselves from needless danger and distress and come to our destination safely and in your grace.

Michael Buckley

### *For Protection*

Protect us, O Lord, from all danger to men that may arise from the difficulties of travelling, the weariness of the body, or from inconsiderate speed, and as, O Lord, you graciously sent the archangel Raphael to be a traveling companion and protector to the young Tobias, so save all your children from all perils of soul and body, so that, journeying along the ways of this world in your sight, they may deserve to reach the haven of eternal salvation. Through Christ our Lord.

Pope John XXIII

### *For Absent Loved Ones*

Almighty Father, you watch over with love the affairs of all your children. Mercifully hear our prayers for those whom we love and from whom we are now parted. Be with them, Lord, and protect them in all the trials of this life. Teach us, and them, to feel and know that you are always near, and that we are never parted from each other if we are united in you through Jesus Christ our Lord.

Michael Buckley

## For Spiritual Growth

### *To Know and Love God*

My God, I love thee: not because
I hope for heaven thereby,
nor yet because who love thee not
are lost eternally.

Thou, O my Jesus, thou didst me
upon the cross embrace;
for me didst bear the nails and spear
and manifold disgrace.
And griefs and torments numberless
and sweat of agony;
even death itself—and all for one
who was thine enemy.

Then why, O blessed Jesu Christ,
should I not love thee well;
not for the sake of winning heaven
or of escaping hell;
not with the hope of gaining aught,
nor seeking a reward:
but as thyself has loved me,
O ever-loving Lord!

so I love thee,
and will love and in thy praise will sing,
solely because thou art my God
and my eternal king.

St. Francis Xavier

***For Strength in Trials***

O Lord, my God, my only hope, hear me, lest through weariness I should not wish to seek you, but may ardently seek your face evermore. Give me the strength to seek, you who have caused me to find you and have given me the hope of finding you more and more.

St. Augustine

***Help Us Come to You***

God, our Father, we find it difficult to come to you,
because our knowledge of you is so imperfect.

In our ignorance we have imagined you to be our enemy;
we have wrongly thought that you take pleasure in
punishing our sins;

and we have foolishly conceived you to be a tyrant over human life.

But since Jesus came among us,
he has shown that you are loving,
that you are on our side against all that stunts life,
and that our resentment against you was groundless.

So we come to you, asking you to forgive our past ignorance, and wanting to know more and more of you and your forgiving love, through Jesus Christ our Lord.

***Prayer of St. Augustine***

Late have I loved you, O beauty so ancient and so new;
late have I loved you.
For behold you were within me, and I outside;
and I sought you outside and in my ugliness fell
upon those lovely things that you have made.
You were with me and I was not with you.
I was kept from you by those things,
yet had they not been in you, they would not have been at all.
You called and cried to me and broke upon my deafness;
and you sent forth your light and shone upon me,
and chased away my blindness;
You breathed fragrance upon me,
and I drew in my breath and do not pant for you:
I tasted you, and I now hunger and thirst for you;
you touched me, and I have burned for your peace.

St. Augustine, *Confessions*

### *A Steadfast Heart*

Give me, O Lord, a steadfast heart, which no unworthy thought can drag downward; an unconquered heart, which no tribulation can wear out; an upright heart, which no unworthy purpose may tempt aside. Bestow upon me also, O Lord my God, understanding to know thee, diligence to seek thee, wisdom to find thee, and a faithfulness that may finally embrace thee, through Jesus Christ, our Lord.

St. Thomas Aquinas

### *Lord, I Seek You*

Lord, where shall I find you?
High and hidden is your place.
And where shall I not find you?
The world is full of your glory.

I have sought your nearness,
With all my heart I called you,
and in going out to meet you
I found you coming in to meet me.

Judah Halevi

### *Raise My Heart*

O my God, give me thy grace so that the things of this earth and things more naturally pleasing to me may not be as close as thou art to me. Keep thou my eyes, my ears, my heart from clinging to the things of this world. Break my bonds, raise my heart. Keep my whole being fixed on thee. Let me never lose sight of thee; and while I gaze on thee, let my love of thee grow more and more every day.

St. John Henry Newman

### *The Grace of Love*

You who are love itself, give me the grace of love, give me yourself, so that all my days may finally empty into the one day of your eternal life.

Karl Rahner

### *By Love Alone*

O God, who by love alone are great and glorious, who are present and live with us by love alone: grant us likewise by love to attain another self, by love to live in others, and by love to come to our glory to see and accompany your love throughout all eternity.

Thomas Traherne

### *Set Us on Fire*

Come, Lord, work upon us, set us on fire and clasp us close, be fragrant to us, draw us to your loveliness, let us love, let us run to you.

St. Augustine

### *Shine Through Me*

Lord, make me like crystal, that your light may shine through me.

Katherine Mansfield

### *Enfold Me*

Lord, enfold me in the depths of your heart; and there hold me, refine, purge, and set me on fire; raise me aloft until my own self knows utter annihilation.

Teilhard de Chardin

### *True Charity*

O Lord God, give me true charity that never fails, so that my life may shine as a light that warms my own heart and gives comfort to others.

St. Columbanus

### *Reign Over Us*

O God, reign over us in spite of our infidelities; may the fire of your love quench every other fire. What can we see that is lovable outside of you, and which we do not find perfectly in you, who are the source of all good? Grant us the grace of loving you; we shall then love you only, and we shall love you eternally.

François Fénelon

### *Worthy of an Infinite Love*

O God, worthy of an infinite love, I have nothing that can adequately measure thy dignity, but such is my desire toward thee that if I had all that thou hast, I would gladly and thankfully resign all to thee.

St. Gertrude

### *Teach Us*

Teach us, O Lord, to fear without being afraid; to fear thee in love that we may love thee without fear; through Jesus Christ our Lord.

Christina Rossetti

### *Let Me Walk in the Way of Love*

O my God, let me walk in the way of love, which knows not how to seek self in anything whatsoever. Let me love thee for thyself, and nothing else but in and for thee. Let me love nothing instead of thee, for to give all for love is a most sweet bargain. Let thy love work in me and by me, and let me love thee as thou wouldst be loved by me.

Dame Gertrude More

***Let Me Know Thee***

Lord Jesus, let me know myself; let me know thee
And desire nothing else but thee.
Let me love myself only if I love thee
And do all things for thy sake.
Let me humble myself and exalt thee
And think of nothing else but thee.
Let me die to myself and live in thee
And take whatever happens as coming from thee.
Let me forsake myself and walk after thee
And ever desire to follow thee.
Let me flee from myself and turn to thee,
That so I may merit to be defended by thee.
Let me fear for myself; let me fear thee
And be among those that are chosen by thee.
Let me distrust myself and trust in thee
And ever obey for the love of thee.
Let me cleave to nothing but thee
And ever be poor because of thee.
Look upon me that I may love thee;
Call me, that I may see thee
And forever possess thee, for all eternity.

St. Augustine

### *To Know You and to Know Myself*

I thank thee, Lord, for knowing me better than I know myself and for letting me know myself better than others know me. Make me, I pray, better than they suppose, and forgive me for what they do not know. Lord Jesus, eternal Word of the Father, who brought us the words of the gospel, grant me through them to know you and to know myself. Show me my wretchedness and your mercy; my sin and your grace; my poverty and your riches; my weakness and your strength; my stupidity and your wisdom; my darkness and your light.

### *For Love of the Bible*

Lord, who can grasp all the wealth of just one of your words? What we understand in the Bible is much less than what we leave behind, like thirsty people who drink from a fountain. For your word has many shades of meaning, just as those who study it have many different points of view. You have colored your words with many hues, so that each person who studies it can see in it what he loves. You have hidden many treasures in your word, so that each of us is enriched as we meditate on it.

St. Ephraim

### *Write Your Word on Our Hearts*

Write upon our hearts, O Lord God, the lessons of thy holy Word, and grant that we all may be doers of the same and not forgetful hearers only.

A. Campbell Fraser

## For the Inner Life

### *For a Spirit of True Prayer*

O Lord God, who never fails both to hear and to answer the prayer that is sincere: let not our hearts be upon the world when our hands are lifted up to pray, nor our prayers end upon our lips but go forth with power to work thy will in the world; through Jesus Christ our Lord.

O God of love, who bids thy children pray, not that thou need to be entreated, but that we may be more capable of blessings by desiring them: make us both to desire and to entreat according to thy will, that we may receive according to thine immeasurable bounty; through Jesus Christ our Lord.

O Lord God, that art a hearer not of the voice but of the heart: Make our prayer that goes up to thee as eager as thy pity that pours down upon us, for Christ's sake.

Dame Gertrude More

### *For a Spirit of Thanksgiving*

God, whose mercy is boundless and whose gifts are without end, help us always to thank you for everything that your loving power has bestowed on us. Make us realize that our desire to thank you is itself your gift and that our thankfulness is never ending because your love is never failing.

Michael Buckley

### *Give Me, O Christ*

Give me, O Christ, the courage of faith. Pierce the hidden depths of my spirit like a two-edged sword. Give me your clear light to guide my conscience. Give me that love that delights me in the seclusion of my timid heart and without which I cannot know you as the Lord of all things, of atoms and stars, of human bodies and spiritual worlds. Then shall I be truly blessed in you, then shall I have my heart's desire and the purpose of my existence.

Hugo Rahner

***Deliver Me***

From the cowardice that dare not face new truth,
From the laziness that is contented with half-truth,
From the arrogance that thinks it knows all truth,
Good Lord, deliver me.

Prayer From Kenya

***Courage to Follow the Shepherd***

May he give us all the courage that we need to go the way he shepherds us, that when he calls we may go unfrightened. If he bids us come to him across the waters, that unfrightened we may go. And if he bids us climb the hill, may we not notice that it is a hill, mindful only of the happiness of his company. He made us for himself, that we should travel with him and see him at last in his unveiled beauty in the abiding city, where he is light and happiness and endless home.

Bede Jarrett

***For Serenity***

God, grant me
the serenity to accept the things I cannot change,
the courage to change the things I can,
and the wisdom to distinguish the one from the other.

Living one day at a time;
Enjoying one moment at a time;
Accepting hardships as the pathway to peace;
Taking, as he did, this sinful world
as it is, not as I would have it;
Trusting that he will make all things right
if I surrender to his will;
That I may be reasonably happy in this life
and supremely happy with him
forever in the next.
Amen.

Reinhold Niebuhr

***For Peace and Guidance***

O God, source of holy desires, right counsels, and just actions, grant to your servants that peace that the world cannot give, so that our hearts may be wholly devoted to your service, and all our days, freed from dread of our enemies, may be passed in quietness under your protection.

Almighty God, you know our necessities before we ask and our ignorance in asking. Set us free from all anxious thoughts for the morrow; give us contentment with your good gifts; and confirm our faith, that as we seek your kingdom, you will not suffer us to lack anything we need through Jesus Christ our Lord.

God, our Father, I turn to you in my unrest, because I cannot see any way out of the present situation that troubles my spirit. In my confusion I turn to you for help and guidance, because you alone can help me, and nothing is impossible to you. Light up my life with faith, strengthen me in hope, and fill me with love, so that I may rest in your providence, which alone knows what is for my peace.

Michael Buckley

***For Inner Silence***

O Christ, my Lord, I pray that you will turn my heart to you in the depths of my being, where with the noise of creatures silenced and the clamor of bothersome thoughts stilled, I shall stay with you where I find you always present.

Fr. Lessius

***Slowing Down***

Slow me down, Lord,
ease the pounding of my heart
by the quieting of my mind.

Teach me the art of slowing down,
to look at a flower,
to chat to a friend,
to read a few lines from a good book.

Remind me each day of the fable
of the hare and the tortoise,
that I may know that the race
is not always to the swift,
that there is more to life than
increasing its speed.
Let me look upward into the
branches of the towering oak

and know that it grew great and
strong because it grew slowly
and well.

Slow me down, Lord, and inspire
me to send my roots deep into
the soil of life's enduring values,
that I may grow toward
the stars of my greater destiny.

Wilferd A. Peterson

## In Times of Trial

### *Strength and Consolation*

Lord Jesus, in times of trial and temptation, be my strength and consolation. Teach me not to fear the darkness, but rather draw me to your light. For it can only be in darkness that you will become my light, and in your light that I may bring the light of healing love to all I meet.

George Maloney

### *In Danger*

Grant, we beseech you, O Lord our God, that in whatever dangers we are placed we may call upon your name, and that when deliverance is given us from on high, we may never cease your praise, through Jesus Christ our Lord.

*Leonine Sacramentary*

### *Victory Over Spiritual Foes*

O Lord, our God, grant us, we beseech you, patience in troubles, humility in comforts, constancy in temptations, and victory over all our spiritual foes. Grant us sorrow for our sins, thankfulness for your benefits, fear of your judgment, love of your mercies, and mindfulness of your presence, now and for ever.

John Cosin

***For Patience in Suffering***

O my dear Lord, though I am not fit to ask thee for suffering as a gift, and have no strength to do so, at least I will beg of thee grace to meet suffering well, when thou in thy love and wisdom dost bring it upon me.

St. John Henry Newman

***When Deprived of Consolation***

Since thou hast taken from me all that I had of thee, yet of thy grace leave that gift which every dog has by nature: that of being true in my distress, when I am deprived of any consolation.

St. Mechtilde

**For Others**

***An Understanding Heart***

Grant me, O Lord, an understanding heart, that I may see into the hearts of your people and know their strengths and weaknesses, their hopes and their despairs, their efforts and failures, their need of love and their need to love. Through my touch with them, grant comfort and hope and the assurance that new life begins at any age and on any day, redeeming the past, sanctifying the present, and brightening the future with the assurance of your unfailing love, brought to me in Jesus

Christ, your Son, my Lord.

George Appleton

***Recognize God in Others***

Grant me to recognize in other men, Lord God, the radiance of your own face.

Teilhard de Chardin

***Help Me to Be Human***

God, help me to be human. Help me to be able to appreciate and bring out the best in everyone around me. You have created man so that he is capable to appreciate consciously all the gifts that you have given him. Lord, help me to appreciate all that you have given me. Help me to be truly human.

Teenagers' Prayer, From Harare, Zimbabwe

***For Respect***

Lord, teach me to respect people, to accept each person as unique and created by you. Some people seem so unattractive that I find it extremely difficult to see you in them. Yet if I could see myself as others see me, perhaps I would be less critical and more understanding. Of your goodness give me compassion for myself and for others, and never let me give up trying, for the sake of your Son, who genuinely loved and cared about sinners and outcasts.

Michael Rollings and Etta Gullick

***Grace to Put Self Aside***

Give us patience and fortitude to put self aside for you in the most unlikely people: to know that every man's and any man's suffering is our own first business, for which we must be willing to go out of our way and to leave our own interests.

Caryll Houselander

***For Unselfishness***

O Lord, do not let us turn into "broken cisterns" that can hold no water. Do not let us be so blinded by the enjoyment of the good things of earth that our hearts become insensitive to the cry of the poor, of the sick, of orphaned children, and of those innumerable brothers of ours who lack the necessary minimum to eat, to clothe their nakedness, and to gather their family together under one roof.

Pope John XXIII

***Unselfish Courage***

Help me, O Lord, so to strive and so to act that those things that cloud my own way may not darken the path that others have to tread. Give me unselfish courage, so that I am ready always to share my bread and wine and yet able to hide my hunger and thirst.

Leslie Weatherhead

***Teach Me How to Love***

Lord, to love is to meet oneself, and to meet oneself one must be willing to leave oneself and go toward another. To love is to commune, and to commune one must forget oneself for another. One must die to self completely for another. Loving hurts, for since the Fall…to love is to crucify self for another. Teach me how to love.

Michel Quoist

***For Respect for Animals***

God, loving Creator of all life, help us to treat with compassion the living creatures entrusted to our care; may they never be subjected to cruelty and neglect, and may the dominion you gave us over them be a partnership of mutual service, so that through them we come to a greater appreciation of your glory in creation.

Michael Buckley

***For Humility***

O God, you reject the proud and welcome the humble. Give us true humility, such as your only-begotten Son showed in himself as a pattern for his followers. May we never provoke your wrath by pride but rather receive your gifts of grace as servants.

***For True Use of Freedom***

God our Father, whose law is a law of liberty, grant us wisdom to use aright the freedom you have given us by surrendering ourselves to your service, knowing that when we are your willing bondsmen, then only are we truly free, for Jesus Christ's sake.

***For Good Use of Talents and Possessions***

Heavenly Father, your Son Jesus Christ has taught us that all our possessions and talents are on trust from you. Help us to be zealous and faithful stewards of all you have given us, so that, true to your grace, we may merit to be welcomed into your kingdom as good and faithful servants, who have in all things sought and accomplished your holy will.

Michael Buckley

### *In Wholehearted Repentance*

Almighty and most gentle God, when your chosen people were thirsty, you drew a stream of water from a rock. From our stony hearts draw tears of sorrow, giving us the grace to weep for our sins and win your merciful forgiveness.

### *For Forgiveness of Sin*

We beseech you, Lord, to listen to our humble prayers: Be merciful toward the sinfulness of us who confess our misdeeds, and in your goodness forgive us and set our minds at rest.

### *For Community Spirit*

O God, teach us to live together in love and joy and peace,
to check all bitterness, to disown discouragement,
to practice thanksgiving,
and to leap with joy to any task for others.
Strengthen the good things thus begun,
that with gallant and high-hearted happiness
we may look for your kingdom in the wills of men.

The Prayer of Toc H

### *Bound Together in Life*

O God, who has bound us together in this bundle of life, give us grace to understand how our lives depend on the courage, the industry, the honesty, and the integrity of our fellow men; that we may be mindful of their needs, grateful for their faithfulness, and faithful in our responsibilities to them; through Jesus Christ our Lord.

Reinhold Niebuhr

### *For Charity*

O God, you make all things work together for the good of those who love you. Kindle the abiding fire of your charity in our hearts, that the longings you inspire in us may not be stifled by any temptation.

### *For Charitable Speech*

Set a watch, Lord, upon our tongue, that we may never speak the cruel word that is not true or, being true, is not the whole truth or, being wholly true, is merciless; for the love of Jesus Christ our Lord.

### *For Compassion*

Give me the grace to be compassionate with sinners from the depths of my heart. May I not be arrogant with them but weep together with them. Grant that, weeping over my neighbor, I may also weep over myself.

## In Times of Sickness and Healing

### *Redemptive Suffering*

O Christ, my Lord, who for my sins did hang upon a tree,
grant that your grace in me, poor wretch, may still ingrafted be.
Grant that your naked hanging there may kill in me all pride
and care of wealth, since you did then in such poor state abide.
Grant that your crown of prickling thorns, which you for me did wear,
may make me willing for your sake all shame and pain to bear.
Grant that your pierced hand, which did of nothing all things frame,

may move me to lift up my hands and ever praise your name.
Grant that your wounded feet, whose steps were perfect evermore,
may learn my feet to tread those paths which you have gone before.
Grant that your blessed grave, wherein your body lay awhile,
may bury all such vain delights as may my mind defile.
Grant, Lord, that your ascending then may lift my mind to thee,
that there my heart and joy may rest, though here in flesh I be.

St. Philip Howard*

***O Tree of Calvary***

O tree of Calvary,
send your roots deep down
into my heart.
Gather together the soil of my heart,
the sands of my fickleness,
the mud of my desires.
Bind them all together,
O tree of Calvary,
interlace them with thy strong roots,
entwine them with the network of thy love.

A Prayer of an Indian Christian

***Facing Pain***

Father, the world is full of pain; each of us has a share; for some it is a slight burden, for others it is crushing. But every

Christian can turn it into a blessing if he will seek the companionship of Christ in his sufferings; then the pain becomes a new point of fellowship with Christ; and even our suffering becomes part of the price of the world's redemption as we fill up what is left over of the suffering of Christ.

Pain does not then cease to be pain; but it ceases to be barren pain; and with fellowship with Christ upon the cross we find new strength for bearing it and even making it the means by which our hearts are more fully cleansed of selfishness and grow toward perfect love. Accomplish this in us through Christ our Lord.

William Temple

***Coping With Pain***

Lord, we do not ask you to rid us of pain, but in your mercy grant that our pain may be free from waste, unfretted by rebellion against your will, unsoiled by thought of ourselves, purified by love of others, and ennobled by devotion to your kingdom through the merits of your only Son, our Lord.

Robert Nash

***Suffering With Jesus***

O crucified Jesus, in giving me your cross, give me too your spirit of love and self-abandonment; grant that I may think less of my suffering than of the happiness of suffering with you. What do I suffer that you have not suffered? Or rather what do I suffer at all, if I dare to compare myself with you? O Lord, grant that I may love you, and then I shall no longer fear the cross.

François Fénelon

### *The Power of Suffering*

Lord, make us realize that by simply suffering for Jesus' sake and by bearing "in the body the death of Jesus" [2 Corinthians 4:10], we can often do more for him and for others than we can by being active. It is very hard to understand this, so please make us realize that our very helplessness can be of great use to others, if we suffer it with and for Jesus.

Our suffering works mysteriously, first in ourselves by a kind of renewal and also in others who are perhaps far away, without our ever knowing what we are accomplishing. Christ on the cross has perhaps done more for humanity than Christ speaking and acting in Galilee or Jerusalem. Suffering creates life. It transforms everything it touches. Help us to understand this through Christ, our Lord.

Elizabeth Leseur

### *The Saving Power of Christ's Resurrection*

Lord Jesus, teach me to realize that all pain is taken up into the saving power of your resurrection, and just as you suffered, even death itself, to the Father's glory, so may my lesser sufferings be one with yours for the salvation of the world.

Michael Buckley

### *For the Help of the Holy Spirit*

Grant, Lord, that as you sent this sickness to me, you will also send your Holy Spirit into my heart so that my present illness may be sanctified and used as a school in which I may learn to know the greatness of my misery and the riches of your mercy. May I be so humbled at my misery that I despair not of your mercy and thus renounce all confidence in myself and every other creature, so that I may put the whole of my salvation in your all-sufficient merits.

Lewis Bayley

### *For Patience in Suffering*

Father,
Your Son accepted our sufferings
to teach us the virtue of patience in human illness.
Hear the prayers we offer for our sick brothers and sisters.
May all who suffer pain, illness, or disease
realize that they are chosen to be saints
and know that they are joined in Christ
in his sufferings for the salvation of the world.

Lord, teach me the art of patience while I am well, and give me the use of it when I am sick. In that day either lighten my burden or strengthen my back. Make me, who so often in my health have discovered my weakness, to be strong in my sickness when I solely rely on your assistance.

Thomas Fuller

### *For Resignation in Illness*

God, you are a loving Father who will not cause us a needless tear; give us then a peaceful heart at rest in the present trouble that afflicts us, and which we offer to you in union with the sufferings of Christ, your Son. May we concentrate more on your love and care rather than on our own selfish preoccupation with physical pain and emotional disturbance. You know the right time to lift the burden that oppresses us, and so we place the present moment, as we do our whole lives, in your tender care. Put your rest in our minds and your peace in our hearts.

Michael Buckley

***Unshaken Will in Affliction***

O good Jesus, I offer and resign myself to you in perfect readiness of will to bear the affliction that I foresee coming upon me. I will accept it with unshaken will as from your hand, and I will bear it with all the patience I can, in union with the love with which you bore all your afflictions as coming from your Father's hand and offered them in gratitude to him. I pray that you would grant me fortitude and patience to bear my suffering with gallantry, to the praise of your eternal glory and the peace of all the world.

St. Gertrude

***For Trust***

O loving Father, we pray for all who are handicapped in the race of life: the blind, the defective and the delicate, and all who are permanently injured. We pray for those worn out with sickness and those who are wasted with misery, for the dying and all unhappy children. May they learn the mystery of the road of suffering, which Christ has trodden and the saints have followed, and bring you this gift that angels cannot bring, a heart that trusts you even in the dark; and this we ask in the name of him who himself took our infirmities upon him, even the same Jesus, our Savior.

A.S.T. Fisher

### *For Those Who Nurse the Sick*

Lord, I thank you that in your love you have taken from me all earthly riches, and that you now clothe and feed me through the kindness of others. Lord, I thank you that, since you have taken from me the sight of my eyes, you serve me now with the eyes of others.

Lord, I thank you that, since you have taken away the power of my hands and my heart, you serve me by the hands and hearts of others. Lord, I pray for them. Reward them…in your heavenly love, that they may faithfully serve and please you till they reach a happy end.

St. Mechtilde

### *For Physicians*

O Lord, the healer of our diseases, who knows that the sick have need of a physician, bless all whom you have called to be sharers in your own work of healing with health alike of body and soul, that they may learn their art in dependence upon you and exercise it always under your sanction and your honor and glory, who live and reign with the Holy Spirit, ever one God, world without end. Amen.

*Sursum Corda*

### *For God's Presence in Suffering*

Father, you do not protect us against catastrophes, but in them you come to our aid. It is in the very midst of the tempest and misfortune that a wonderful zone of peace, serenity, and joy bursts in us if we dwell in your grace. You do not help us before we have helped ourselves, but when we are at the end of our resources, you manifest yourself, and we begin to know that you have been there all the time.

Louis Evely

### *In Failing Health and Old Age*

When the signs of age begin to mark my body and still more when they touch my mind; when the illness that is to diminish me or carry me off strikes from without or is born within me; when the painful moment comes in which I suddenly awaken to the fact that I am ill or growing old; in all those dark moments, O God, grant that I may understand that it is you, provided only my faith is strong enough, who are painfully parting the fibers of my being in order to penetrate to the very marrow of my substance and bear me away within yourself.

Teilhard de Chardin

### *For Healing*

Lord, heal your servants who are sick and put their trust in you.

**Send them help, O Lord, and comfort from your holy place.**

Let us pray:
Almighty and everlasting God, the eternal salvation of those who believe in you, hear us on behalf of your servants who are sick, for whom we humbly beg the help of your mercy. May their health be restored if you see that it is good for them, and may they give you thanks in your Church.
Through Christ our Lord.

**Amen.**

### *The Healing Power of the Holy Name*

Jesus, your coming on earth was like a new dawn over a world of darkness: The blind saw, the lame walked again, the sick were healed, and even the dead were raised to life. Come again into the lives of everyone, and heal the wounds of their broken hearts. Come again to all who are sick or depressed, and fill their lives with hope and peace. Come again to us as we call on your holy name, so that we too may receive your help and healing grace.

Michael Buckley

### *Healer of a Wounded World*

God, our Father, you sent your only Son Jesus…to heal a brokenhearted and wounded world. He had compassion on those who called on him for help and healing. He touched the sick and guilt-laden, and they walked away in health and freedom of Spirit. Visit us now with his saving power, so that we too may be released in mind and body to praise your healing grace through Christ our Lord.

Michael Buckley

### *Healing Grace*

God, we witness unheard of things. You, God, have given power to Jesus of Nazareth, whom we recognize as one of us, to be merciful to others and to forgive them. We ask you, God, for this power, this freedom to be a healing grace to all who live in this world, as a sign that you are the forgiveness of sins.

*A Christian's Prayer Book*

### *True Health of Mind and Body*

God, our Father, your Son gave more than he was asked for to those who pleaded with him for healing. People asked for health of body, and he released them from their sins as well; he touched their skin and healed the deep wounds of the spirit. May we be touched by the same healing power and thus be released from the hidden forces deep within us that hold us back from true health of mind and body.

Michael Buckley

### *Great Friend of the Sick*

Lord Jesus, you are the great friend of the sick,
and you healed them while you were on earth.
Grant them once more your healing power,
  and comfort them in their affliction.
Come, Holy Spirit, strengthen them
  so that they may find renewed health
  both in soul and body.

### *For Healing Sleep*

Lord Jesus Christ, who slept on a storm-tossed lake, grant me the gift of sleep, so that with a mind at peace, a heart at rest, and a body relaxed, I may use my sleeping hours for healing and waken strengthened to renew my tasks with brighter vision, confidence, and hope.

Michael Buckley

### *A Blessing for the Sick*

Lord Jesus, when you were on earth, they brought the sick to you, and you healed them all. Today we ask you to bless all

those in sickness, in weakness, and in pain;
Those who are blind and who cannot see the light of the sun, the beauty of the world, or the faces of their friends;
those who are deaf and cannot hear the voices that speak to them;
those who are helpless and who must lie in bed while others go out and in.

*Bless all such.*

Those whose minds have lost their reason;
those who are so nervous that they cannot cope with life;
those who worry about everything.

*Bless all such.*

Those who must face life under some handicap;
those whose weakness means that they must always be careful;
those who are lame and maimed and cannot enter into any of the strenuous activities or pleasures of life.

*Bless all such.*

Grant that we in our health and our strength may never find those who are weak and handicapped a nuisance, but grant that we may always do and give all that we can to help them and to make life easier for them.

William Barclay

***Act of Resignation to Death***

O Lord, my God, I now at this moment, readily and willingly, accept at your hand whatever kind of death it may please you to send me, with all its pains and sorrows. Through Christ, Our Lord. Amen.

Lord Jesus, today we accept from your merciful hands what is to come. The times of trial in this world, the suffering of our death, the sorrow and loneliness of our last hours upon earth, the purifying, unknown pains of our purgatory. Into your hands, O Lord, into your hands we commit our living and dying, knowing that you are the dawn of eternal day, the burning light of the morning star.

Caryll Houselander

***For the Dying***

O most merciful Jesus, lover of souls: I pray you, by the agony of your most Sacred Heart and by the sorrows of your Immaculate Mother, cleanse in your own blood the sinners of the whole world who are now in their agony and are to die this day. May they be comforted by the hope of the Resurrection. Heart of Jesus, once in agony, pity the dying.

Jesus, I ask you to pour down your blessing on the dying. Give them grace to bear their sickness and strength to conform themselves to your blessed will. Pity them and help them by your mercy, that in the final hour they may not lose courage but may have fortitude to fight the good fight for you to the end.

God of power and mercy,
you have made death itself
the gateway to eternal life.
Look with love on our dying brother (sister),
and make him (her) one with your Son in his
sufferings and death,

that sealed with the blood of Christ,
he (she) may come before you free from sin.

### *For Final Perseverance*

Grant, we beseech you, O Lord, that in the hour of our death we may be refreshed by your holy sacraments and delivered from all guilt, and so deserve to be received with joy into the arms of your mercy.

Mother of Sorrows, by the anguish and love with which you stood beneath the cross of Jesus, stand by me in my last moments. To your maternal heart I commend the last hours of my life; offer these hours to the eternal Father in union with the passion of our dearest Lord. Offer frequently, in atonement for my sins, and in gratitude for the Resurrection, the precious blood of Jesus, shed on Calvary, to obtain for me the grace to receive Holy Communion before my death and to breathe forth my soul in the actual presence of Jesus in the Blessed Sacrament; and when the moment of my death has at length arrived, and I stand on the threshold of heaven, present me as your child to Jesus; say to him on my behalf, "Father, receive him (her) this day into your kingdom."
Jesus, I live for you;
Jesus, I die for you;
Jesus, I am yours in life and in death.

### *At Judgment Time*

Have pity upon every man, Lord, in that hour when he has finished his task and stands before thee like a child whose hands are being examined.

Paul Claudel

## PRAYERS TO MARY, MOTHER OF THE CHURCH

*Mary has always had a special place in Christian devotion, perhaps nowhere more pronounced than in the Eastern Church. The reason* all generations shall call her blessed *is that God chose her to be the mother of his Son. By her obedience to his will, she set in physical motion the work of our redemption. The Word was made flesh in her, and mankind was once more restored to God's favor. Mother of the physical body of Jesus Christ, she is also the spiritual Mother of the Church, a title given to her by the bishops of the Second Vatican Council. We honor her and ask her intercession because of her unique relationship with God the Father and Holy Spirit through her Son.*

**Prayers to Our Lady**

***Hail, Holy Queen***

Hail, holy Queen, Mother of Mercy.
Hail, our life, our sweetness, and our hope.
To thee do we cry, poor banished children of Eve;
to thee do we send up our sighs, mourning and weeping in this vale of tears.
Turn then, most gracious advocate, thine eyes of mercy toward us;
and after this our exile, show unto us the blessed fruit of thy womb, Jesus.
O clement, O loving, O sweet virgin Mary.
Pray for us, O holy Mother of God.

**That we may be made worthy of the promises of Christ.**

Let us pray:
Almighty, everlasting God, who through the working of the Holy Spirit prepared the body and soul of the glorious Virgin Mary to be a worthy dwelling for thy Son, grant that we who remember her with joy may be delivered by her prayers from the evils that beset us in this world and from everlasting death in the next. Through the same Christ our Lord.

**Amen.**

***The Memorare***

Remember, O most loving Virgin Mary, that never was it known that anyone who fled to your protection, implored your help, or sought your intercession was left unaided.
Inspired by this confidence, we fly unto you,
O Virgin of virgins, our mother.
To you we come, before you we stand, sinful and sorrowful.
O Mother of the Word Incarnate, despise not our petitions,
but in your mercy hear and answer us. Amen.

St. Bernard

***The Angelus***

The angel of the Lord declared unto Mary:

**And she conceived of the Holy Spirit.**

Hail Mary…
Behold the handmaid of the Lord:

**Be it done unto me according to your word.**

Hail Mary…
*All genuflect at the following words:*
And the Word was made flesh:

**And dwelt among us.**

*All rise.*

Hail Mary…

Pray for us, O Holy Mother of God

**That we may be made worthy of the promises of Christ.**

Let us pray:

Pour forth, we beseech you, O Lord, your grace into our hearts, that we to whom the incarnation of Christ, your Son, was made known by the message of an angel, may be brought by his passion and cross to the glory of his resurrection, through the same Christ our Lord.

**Amen.**

May the divine assistance remain always with us, and may the souls of the faithful departed, through the mercy of God, rest in peace.

**Amen.**

***Regina Coeli***

*Said in Paschal Time*

O Queen of heaven, rejoice! Alleluia.

For he whom you did merit to bear, Alleluia.

Has risen as he said. Alleluia.

Pray for us to God. Alleluia.

Rejoice and be glad, O Virgin Mary, Alleluia.

**For the Lord has risen indeed. Alleluia.**

Let us pray:
O God, who gave joy to the world through the resurrection of your Son our Lord Jesus Christ, grant that we may obtain, through his virgin mother, Mary, the joys of everlasting life. Through the same Christ our Lord.
**Amen.**

### *For the Conversion of Our Nation*

O blessed Virgin Mary, Mother of God, and our most gentle queen and mother, look down in mercy upon our nation and upon us all who greatly hope and trust in you.

By you it was that Jesus, our Savior and our hope, was given to the world; he has given you to us that we might hope still more. Plead for us your children, whom you did receive and accept at the foot of the cross, O Sorrowful Mother.

Intercede for our separated brothers and sisters, that with us in the one true fold, they may be united to the chief shepherd, the vicar of your Son. Pray for us all, dear Mother, that by faith fruitful in good works, we may all deserve to see and praise God, together with you, in our heavenly home. Amen.

### *To Our Lady of Perpetual Succor*

Most holy Virgin Mary, who, to inspire me with boundless confidence, has been pleased to take that name, Mother of Perpetual Succor, I beseech you to aid me at all times and in all places: in my temptations, in my difficulties, in all the miseries of life, and above all at the hour of my death, so that I may share in the resurrection of your Son our Lord Jesus Christ. Grant, most charitable Mother, that I may remember you at all times and always have recourse to you; for I am sure that, if I am faithful in invoking you, you will promptly come to my aid. Obtain for me, therefore, the grace to pray to you unceasingly with filial confidence, that by virtue of this constant prayer, I may obtain your perpetual help and persevere in the practice of my faith. Bless me, most tender Mother, ever ready to aid me, and pray for me now and at the hour of my death.

Mother of Perpetual Succor, protect also all those whom I recommend to you: the Church, the Holy Father, our country, my family, my friends and enemies, especially all those who suffer.

### *To Our Lady of Good Counsel*

Most glorious virgin, chosen by the eternal counsel to be the mother of the eternal Word made flesh, treasure of divine grace and advocate of sinners, I, the most unworthy of your servants, beseech you to be my guide and counselor in this vale of tears. Obtain for me, by the most precious blood of your Son, the pardon of my sins, the salvation of my soul, and the means necessary to obtain it. Grant that the holy Catholic Church may triumph over the enemies of the gospel and that the kingdom of Christ may be propagated on earth.

### *To Our Lady of Lourdes*

Ever immaculate Virgin, Mother of mercy, health of the sick, refuge of sinners, comfort of the afflicted, you know my needs, my troubles, my sufferings; cast on me a look of pity.

By appearing in the grotto of Lourdes, you were pleased to make it a privileged sanctuary from which you dispense your favors, and already many sufferers have obtained the cure of their infirmities, both spiritual and physical. I come, therefore, with unbounded confidence to implore your maternal intercession. Obtain, most loving Mother, my requests, through Jesus Christ your Son, our Lord. Amen.

***The Ave Maria of St. Mechtilde***

*Hail,* thou unique offspring of the omnipotence of the Father, of the wisdom of the Son, and of the goodness of the Holy Spirit, *Mary,* who dost fill heaven and earth with thy gentle light. Thou that art *full of grace, the Lord is with thee,* even the only-begotten Son of the Father, and the one only Son of the love of thy virgin heart, thy sweetest spouse and thy beloved. *Blessed art thou among women,* for thou hast banished the curse of Eve and hast brought back an everlasting blessing. *And blessed is the fruit of thy womb, Jesus,* the Lord and Creator of all things, who doth evermore bless and sanctify, enrich and give life to all things.

***Mary's Generous Help***

Holy Mary, succor the wretched, help the disheartened, put new heart into the feeble. Pray for the people, intervene for the clergy, intercede for all holy women. May all those who honor your memory experience your generous help. Promptly you attend to the voice of those who pray to you and satisfy the desire of each one. Let your undertaking be diligent intercession for the people of God, for you have merited to bear the ransom of the world, he who lives and reigns for ever.

Fulbert of Chartres

### *A Faithful Disciple*

O Mary, help me to live as a faithful disciple of Jesus, for the building up of Christian society and the joy of the Catholic Church. I greet you, Mother, morning and evening; I pray to you as I go upon my way; from you I hope for the inspiration and encouragement that will enable me to fulfill the sacred promises of my earthly vocation, give glory to God, and win eternal salvation, O Mary! Like you in Bethlehem and on Golgotha, I too wish to stay always close to Jesus. He is the eternal King of all ages and all peoples.

Pope John XXIII

### *The Soul and Spirit of Mary*

O, that the soul of Mary were in us to glorify the Lord! That the spirit of Mary were in us to rejoice in God.

St. Ambrose

### *Thirty Days Prayer to the Blessed Virgin Mary in Honor of the Sacred Passion of Our Lord Jesus Christ*

*It has long been a custom in the Church to say this prayer of petition on thirty consecutive days. It is also recommended as a Lenten devotion as well as for all Fridays throughout the year, because it concentrates on our Lord's saving passion.*

Ever glorious and blessed Mary, Queen of Virgins, Mother of Mercy, through that sword of sorrow that pierced your tender heart while your only Son, Jesus Christ, our Lord, suffered death and ignominy on the cross; through that filial tenderness and pure love he has for you, while from his cross he recommended you to the care and protection of his beloved disciple, St. John, take pity, I beseech you, on my poverty and need; have compassion on my anxieties and cares; assist and comfort me in all my infirmities and miseries. You are the mother of mercies, the only refuge of the needy and the orphan, of the desolate and afflicted.

Cast therefore an eye of pity on this sorrowful child of Eve, and hear my prayer; for since, in just punishment of my sins, I find myself surrounded by a multitude of evils and oppressed with much anguish of spirit, where can I fly for more secure shelter, O loving mother of my Lord and Savior Jesus Christ, than under the wings of your maternal protection? Listen, therefore, I beseech you, with an air of pity and compassion, to my humble and earnest request.

I ask it through the infinite mercy of your dear Son: through that love and humility with which he embraced our human nature, when through your own obedience to the divine will you consented to become his mother, and whom after nine months you brought forth from your chaste womb, to visit this world and bless it with his presence. I ask it through the anguish of mind of your beloved Son, our dear Savior, on Mount Olivet, when he besought his eternal Father to remove from him, if possible, the bitter chalice of his future passion. I ask it through the threefold repetition of his prayers in the garden, from whence afterward in sorrow you accompanied him to the scene of his death and sufferings.

I ask it through the laceration of his sinless flesh, caused by the cords and whips with which he was bound and scourged when stripped of his seamless garments, for which his executioners afterward cast lots. I ask it through the scoffs and ignominies by which he was insulted; the false accusations and unjust sentence by which he was condemned to death and which he bore with enduring patience. I ask it through his bitter tears and bloody sweat; his silence and resignation; his sadness and grief of heart.

I ask it through the blood that trickled from his royal and sacred head, when struck with the scepter of a reed and pierced with his crown of thorns. I ask it through the excruciating torments he suffered, when his hands and feet were fastened with nails to the tree of the cross. I ask it through his unbearable thirst and bitter potion of vinegar and gall. I ask it through his dereliction on the cross, when he exclaimed: *My God, my God, why have you forsaken me?* I ask it through his mercy extended to the good thief and through his recommending his precious soul and spirit into the hands of his eternal Father before he expired, saying: *All is consummated.* I ask it through the blood mixed with water, which issued from his sacred side when pierced with a lance and from whence a flood of grace and mercy has flowed to us.

I ask it through his immaculate life, bitter passion, and ignominious death on the cross, at which even nature itself was thrown into convulsions by the bursting of rocks, rending of the veil of the temple, earthquake, and darkness of the sun and moon. I ask it through his glorious victory over death, when he arose again to life on the third day, and through the joy that his appearance for forty days gave you, his blessed mother, his apostles, and the rest of his disciples, when in your and their presence he miraculously ascended into heaven.

I ask it through the grace of the Holy Spirit, infused into the hearts of his disciples when he descended upon them in the form of fiery tongues, and by which they were inspired with zeal for the conversion of the world when they went to preach the gospel. I ask it through the glorious appearance of your Son at the last day, when he shall come to judge the living and the dead and the world by fire. I ask it through the compassion he bore you in this life and the wonderful joy you felt at your assumption into heaven, where you eternally contemplate his divine perfection.

O glorious and ever Blessed Virgin, comfort the heart of your suppliant by obtaining for me

*Here mention or reflect on your request.*

And as I believe that my divine Savior honors you as his beloved mother, to whom he refuses nothing, because you ask nothing contrary to his honor, so let me soon experience your powerful intercession. Wherefore, O most Blessed Virgin, beside my present petition, and whatever else I may stand in need of, obtain for me also of your dear Son, our Lord and our God, a lively faith, firm hope, perfect charity, true contrition of heart and genuine tears of compunction, sincere confession, satisfaction and deliverance from sin, love of God and my neighbor, a correct attitude toward the world, patience to suffer insults, even death itself, for love of your Son, our Savior Jesus Christ. Obtain likewise for me, O holy Mother of God, perseverance in good works, the carrying out of my good resolutions, mortification of my self-will, a holy life, and at my last moments, a strong and sincere repentance, with such presence of mind as will enable me to receive the last sacrament of the Church worthily, so as to die in God's friendship and favor.

Lastly I beseech you, for the souls of my parents, brethren, relatives, and benefactors, both living and dead, life everlasting from the only giver of every good and perfect gift, the Lord God almighty, to whom be all power, now and for ever. Amen.

**The Rosary**

*An integral part of Catholic devotional practice since before the thirteenth century, the rosary recalls the principal mysteries of our salvation in groups of five decades (chaplets). Each group of five decades is preceded by the recitation of the Creed and three Hail Marys for an increase in faith, hope, and charity. Each decade may conclude with the recitation of one of the anthems to Our Lady appropriate to the liturgical season or one of the Fatima Prayers (see p. 286). The repetition of the prayers of each decade—one Our Father, ten Hail Marys, and one Glory Be to the Father—helps us meditate on God's love for us.*

Come, Holy Spirit, fill the hearts of the faithful, and kindle in them the fire of your love.
Send forth your Spirit.

**And you will renew the face of the earth.**

Let us pray:

O God, who taught the hearts of the faithful by the light of the Holy Spirit, grant that, by the gift of the same Spirit, we may be always truly wise and ever rejoice in his consolation. Through Christ our Lord.

**Amen.**

***The Joyful Mysteries***

*Usually said on Mondays and Saturdays*

1: The Annunciation

Let us contemplate in this mystery how the angel Gabriel saluted our Blessed Lady with the title "Full of Grace" and made known to her that she had been chosen to be Mother of Our Lord and Savior, Jesus Christ.

Our Father (once), Hail Mary (ten times). Glory Be to the Father (once), and optional anthem follow each mystery.

2: The Visitation

Let us contemplate in this mystery how the Blessed Virgin Mary, having learned from the angel that her cousin Elizabeth had conceived, went with haste into the hill country to visit her and remained with her about three months.

3: The Nativity

Let us contemplate in this mystery how the Blessed Virgin Mary with joy brought forth our Lord Jesus Christ, wrapped him in swaddling clothes, and laid him in a manger, because there was no room for them in the inn at Bethlehem.

4: The Presentation

Let us contemplate in this mystery how, on the day of her purification, the Blessed Virgin Mary, with Joseph, presented the child Jesus in the temple, where holy Simeon joyfully received him into his arms and, with the prophetess Anna, proclaimed him Savior of the world.

5: The Finding of Jesus in the Temple

Let us contemplate in this mystery how the Blessed Virgin Mary and Joseph, having lost the child Jesus in Jerusalem, sought him for three days and to their great joy found him in the temple, sitting in the midst of the doctors, listening to them, and asking them questions.

***The Luminous Mysteries***

*Usually said on Thursdays*

1: The Baptism of Jesus

Let us contemplate in this mystery how Jesus humbled himself to be baptized by John in the Jordan River, and let us consider the Father's words: "You are my beloved Son; with you I am well pleased" (Mark 1:11).

2: The Wedding at Cana

Let us contemplate in this mystery how Jesus responded to the request of his mother and the needs of a young couple, providing the best wine for the marriage feast.

3: The Proclamation of the Kingdom

Let us contemplate in this mystery the riches of the kingdom, as well as the love of our Savior in tenderly teaching us how to please the Father and our own responsibility to live and spread his message of salvation.

4: The Transfiguration
Let us contemplate in this mystery the manifestation of Jesus to his disciples—and to us—as the Son of God and the promised Messiah.

5: The Institution of the Eucharist
Let us contemplate in this mystery the great love of our Savior in giving us his own Body and Blood, that we might be one with him and the Father.

***The Sorrowful Mysteries***
*Usually said on Tuesdays and Fridays*
1: The Agony in the Garden
Let us contemplate in this mystery how our Lord Jesus Christ was so afflicted for us in the garden of Gethsemane that his sweat became as drops of blood trickling to the ground.

2: The Scourging of Jesus
Let us contemplate in this mystery how our Lord Jesus Christ was, by Pilate's most unjust and cruel sentence, bound to a pillar and scourged.

3: The Crowning With Thorns
Let us contemplate in this mystery how Pilate's soldiers clothed our Lord Jesus Christ in purple, plaited a crown of thorns for his head, and bowed before him in mockery.

4: The Carrying of the Cross

Let us contemplate in this mystery how our Lord Jesus Christ, having been sentenced to die, patiently bore the cross that was laid upon him for his torment and ignominy.

5: The Crucifixion

Let us contemplate in this mystery how our Lord Jesus Christ, having come to Calvary, was stripped of his clothes, endured three hours of agony, and expired in the presence of his most afflicted mother.

***The Glorious Mysteries***

*Usually said on Wednesdays and Sundays*

1: The Resurrection

Let us contemplate in this mystery how our Lord Jesus Christ, triumphing gloriously over death, rose again on the third day, immortal and never to suffer again.

2: The Ascension

Let us contemplate in this mystery how our Lord Jesus Christ, forty days after his resurrection, ascended into heaven, in the sight of his holy mother and of his apostles and disciples, to be seated at the right hand of the Father.

3: The Descent of the Holy Spirit

Let us contemplate in this mystery how our Lord Jesus Christ sent, as he had promised, the Holy Spirit upon his apostles after they had persevered in prayer with the Blessed Virgin Mary.

4: The Assumption

Let us contemplate in this mystery how the Blessed Virgin Mary, having passed out of this world, was assumed both body and soul into heaven by her divine Son.

5: The Coronation of Our Lady

Let us contemplate in this mystery how the Blessed Virgin Mary, amid the great jubilee and exultation of the whole court of heaven, was crowned by her divine Son with the brightest diadem of glory.

*If the Litany of Loreto is not said, the rosary is concluded as follows:*

***Hail, Holy Queen***

Hail, holy queen, Mother of mercy;
hail, our life, our sweetness, and our hope;
to thee do we cry, poor banished children of Eve;
to thee do we send up our sighs, mourning and weeping in this valley of tears.
Turn then, most gracious advocate,
thine eyes of mercy toward us;
and after this our exile, show unto us the blessed fruit of thy womb, Jesus.
O clement, O loving, O sweet Virgin Mary.
Queen of the most holy rosary, pray for us.

**That we may be made worthy of the promises of Christ.**

Let us pray:

O God, whose only-begotten Son, by his life, death, and resurrection, has purchased for us the rewards of eternal life, grant, we beseech you, that meditating upon these mysteries in the most holy rosary of the Blessed Virgin Mary, we may both imitate what they contain and obtain what they promise, through the same Christ our Lord. Amen.

***The Prayers of Fatima***

*These prayers can be recited after each decade of the rosary:*

O my Jesus, forgive us our sins, save us from the fires of hell. Lead all souls to heaven, especially those in greatest need.

*When offering a penance:*

O Jesus, it is for your love, for the conversion of sinners, and in reparation for the sins committed against the Immaculate Heart of Mary.

My God, I believe, I adore, I hope, and I love you. I ask pardon for those who do not believe, do not adore, do not hope, and do not love you.

***The Litany of Our Lady (Litany of Loreto)***

Lord, have mercy.

Lord, have mercy.

Christ, have mercy.

Christ, have mercy.

Lord, have mercy.

Lord, have mercy.

Christ, hear us.

Christ, graciously hear us.

God the Father of heaven,
have mercy on us.
God the Son, Redeemer of the world,
have mercy on us.
God the Holy Spirit,
have mercy on us.
Holy Trinity, one God,
have mercy on us.
Holy Mary,
pray for us.
Holy Mother of God,
pray for us.
Holy Virgin of virgins,
pray for us.
Mother of Christ,
pray for us.
Mother of divine grace,
pray for us.
Mother most pure,
pray for us.
Mother most chaste,
pray for us.
Mother inviolate,
pray for us.
Mother undefiled,
pray for us.
Mother most lovable,
pray for us.

Mother most admirable,
pray for us.
Mother of good counsel,
pray for us.
Mother of our Creator,
pray for us.
Mother of our Savior,
pray for us.
Virgin most prudent,
pray for us.
Virgin most venerable,
pray for us.
Virgin most renowned,
pray for us.
Virgin most powerful,
pray for us.
Virgin most merciful,
pray for us.
Virgin most faithful,
pray for us.
Mirror of Justice,
pray for us.
Seat of Wisdom,
pray for us.
Cause of our joy,
pray for us.
Spiritual Vessel,
pray for us.

Vessel of honor,

pray for us.

Singular vessel of devotion,

pray for us.

Mystical Rose,

pray for us.

Tower of David,

pray for us.

Tower of Ivory,

pray for us.

House of Gold,

pray for us.

Ark of the Covenant,

pray for us.

Gate of Heaven,

pray for us.

Morning Star,

pray for us.

Health of the sick,

pray for us.

Refuge of sinners,

pray for us.

Comfort of the afflicted,

pray for us.

Help of Christians,

pray for us.

Queen of patriarchs,

pray for us.

Queen of prophets,
pray for us.
Queen of apostles,
pray for us.
Queen of martyrs,
pray for us.
Queen of confessors,
pray for us.
Queen of virgins,
pray for us.
Queen of all saints,
pray for us.
Queen conceived without original sin,
pray for us.
Queen assumed into heaven,
pray for us.
Queen of the Most Holy Rosary,
pray for us.
Queen of Peace,
pray for us.
Lamb of God, you take away the sins of the world,
spare us, O Lord.
Lamb of God, you take away the sins of the world,
graciously hear us, O Lord.
Lamb of God, you take away the sins of the world,
have mercy on us.
Pray for us, O holy Mother of God,
that we may be worthy of
the promises of Christ.

Let us pray:
Grant that we your servants, Lord, may enjoy unfailing health of mind and body, and through the prayers of the ever Blessed Virgin Mary in her glory, free us from our sorrows in this world and give us eternal happiness in the next. Through Christ our Lord.

Amen.

## PRAYERS TO THE ANGELS AND SAINTS

*The Church militant on earth is linked through Christ's resurrection with the Church triumphant in heaven. We ask the saints' and angels' help in our earthly pilgrimage so that we too one day may share their glory and destiny. We pray especially for the intercession of our patrons, the saints whose names were given to us in baptism.*

### *Thanksgiving for the Saints*

We thank you, God, for the saints of all ages: for those who in times of darkness kept the lamp of faith burning; for the great souls who saw visions of larger truths and dared to declare them; for the multitude of quiet, gracious souls whose presence purified and sanctified the world; and for those known and loved by us, who have passed from this earthly fellowship into the fuller life with you. Accept this our thanksgiving through Jesus Christ, to whom be praise and dominion forever. Amen.

*Fellowship Litanies*

### *For a Share With the Saints*

O God our Father,
source of all holiness,
the work of your hands is manifest in your saints;
the beauty of your truth is reflected in their faith.
May we, who aspire to have part in their joy,
be filled with the Spirit that blessed their lives,
so that, having shared their faith on earth,
we may also know their peace in your kingdom.

*St. Joseph*

To you, O blessed Joseph, we fly in our tribulation, and after imploring the help of your most holy spouse, we ask also with confidence for your patronage. By the affection that united you to the Immaculate Virgin, Mother of God, and the paternal love with which you embraced the child Jesus, we beseech you to look kindly upon the inheritance that Jesus Christ acquired by his precious blood, and by your powerful aid to help us in our needs.

Protect, most careful guardian of the Holy Family, the chosen people of Jesus Christ. Keep us, most loving father, from all pestilence of error and corruption. Be mindful of us, most powerful protector, from your place in heaven, in this warfare with the powers of darkness; and as you did snatch the child Jesus from danger of death, so now defend the holy Church of God from the snares of the enemy and from all adversity. Guard each one of us by your perpetual patronage, so that sustained by your example and help, we may live in holiness, die a holy death, and obtain the everlasting happiness of heaven. Amen.

God, who was pleased to elect blessed Joseph as spouse of your Mother, grant, we beseech you, that as we venerate him as our protector on earth, we may deserve to have him as our intercessor in heaven. You live and reign, world without end. Amen.

O glorious St. Joseph, remind all who work that they are not alone in their labor, their joy, or their sufferings, because Jesus is by their side, with Mary, his mother and ours, supporting them, wiping the sweat from their brows and setting a value on their toil. Teach them to use their labor, as you did, as a supreme means of attaining holiness.

Pope John XXIII

***Prayer to St. Joseph the Workman***

Glorious St. Joseph, model of all who are devoted to labor, obtain for me the grace to work conscientiously, putting the call of duty above my selfish interests, to work with gratitude and joy, considering it an honor to employ and develop, by means of labor, the gifts received from God; to work with order, peace, moderation, and patience without ever recoiling before weariness or difficulties; to work, above all, with purity of intention and with detachment from self, as Jesus worked at Nazareth under the direction of your guidance and skill. Amen.

***For the Help of the Saints***

May holy Mary, and all the saints, intercede for us this day with the Lord, that we may be helped and protected by him who lives and reigns forever and ever.

***To St. Joseph***

Guardian of virgins and holy father Joseph, to whose faithful custody Christ Jesus, innocence itself, and Mary, virgin of virgins, were committed; I ask your prayers that I may, with spotless mind, pure heart, and chaste body, ever serve Jesus and Mary all the days of my life.

### *To a Patron Saint*

O heavenly patron, whose name I rejoice to bear, pray for me always before the throne of God; strengthen me in my faith; confirm me in virtue; defend me in the fight, that being conqueror over the evil one I may deserve to obtain everlasting glory.

### *Prayer to My Guardian Angel*

Angel of God, my guardian dear,
To whom his love commits me here,
Ever this day be at my side,
To light and rule, to guard and guide.

### *St. Peter*

All-powerful Father,
you have built your Church
on the rock of St. Peter's confession of faith.
May nothing divide or weaken
our unity in faith and love.

### *St. Paul*

Glorious St. Paul, who from a persecutor of the Christian name became an apostle of burning zeal, and who, in order that Jesus Christ might be known to the furthermost bounds of the earth, suffered imprisonment, scourging, stoning, shipwreck, and every kind of persecution, and who finally shed your blood to the last drop, obtain for us the grace of accepting, as divine favors, the infirmities, torments, and calamities of this life, so that we may not be drawn from the service of God by the trials of this our exile, but on the contrary may prove ourselves more and more faithful and fervent. Amen.

Pray for us, St. Paul the apostle.

**That we may be made worthy of the promises of Christ.**

Let us pray:
God, who taught the whole world by the preaching of blessed Paul the apostle, grant, we beseech you, that we who celebrate his conversion may feel the might of his intercession before you. Through Christ our Lord. Amen.

***Prayer of St. Michael the Archangel***

Holy Michael the archangel, defend us in the day of battle; be our safeguard against the wickedness and snares of the devil. May God rebuke him, we humbly pray; and may the prince of the heavenly host, by the power of God, thrust down to hell Satan and all wicked spirits, who wander through the world for the ruin of souls. Amen.

***St. Augustine of Hippo***

Glorious St. Augustine, look upon me with compassion, and pray for me to be a worthy child of God our loving Father. Let me say with you: *Too late have I known you, too late have I loved you,* so that I may repair my past sinful life by the most ardent, generous love for my divine spouse. Ask for me a share in your profound humility, that I may ever be little and humble in my eyes, preferring to be made of little account in order to resemble him who underwent such deep humiliations for the love of me. Obtain also for me unbounded courage and confidence, patience, and kindness. At the hour of death, may I go home to my heavenly Father in your dear company, and there may we praise almighty God for all eternity. Amen.

***St. Anthony of Padua***

Holy St. Anthony, gentlest of saints, your love for God and charity toward his creatures made you worthy to possess miraculous powers. Miracles waited on your word, which you were ever ready to speak for those in trouble or anxiety. Encouraged by this thought, I implore of you to obtain for me.... The answer to my prayer may require a miracle; even so, you are the saint of miracles. O gentle and loving St. Anthony, whose heart was ever full of human sympathy, whisper my petition into the ears of the sweet infant Jesus, who loved to be folded in your arms.

***St. Jude***

St. Jude, glorious apostle, faithful servant and friend of Jesus, the name of the man who betrayed our Savior has caused you to be forgotten by many. The Church, however, invokes you as the patron of things despaired of. Pray for me that I may receive the consolations and the help of heaven in all my necessities, tribulations, and sufferings, particularly..., and that I may bless God with the elect throughout eternity. Amen.

***St. Martin de Porres***

Most humble St. Martin, your wonderful love for all who turned to you in need inspires me now to ask your help. I implore you to help me in my present difficulties. I particularly ask you to obtain for me from God.... May I, by imitating your love and humility, find true peace in my life and perfect resignation to the will of God.

### *The Litany of the Saints*

Lord, have mercy on us.
Lord, have mercy on us.
Christ, have mercy on us.
Christ, have mercy on us.
Christ, hear us.
Christ, graciously hear us.
God, the Father of heaven,
have mercy on us.
God the Son, Redeemer of the world,
have mercy on us.
God the Holy Spirit,
have mercy on us.
Holy Trinity, one God,
have mercy on us.
Holy Mary,
pray for us.
Mother of God,
pray for us.
Holy Virgin of virgins,
pray for us.
St. Michael,
pray for us.

St. Gabriel,

pray for us.

St. Raphael,

pray for us.

All holy angels and archangels,

pray for us.

All holy orders of blessed spirits,

pray for us.

St. John the Baptist,

pray for us.

St. Joseph,

pray for us.

All holy patriarchs and prophets,

pray for us.

St. Peter,

pray for us.

St. Paul,

pray for us.

St. Andrew,

pray for us.

St. James,

pray for us.

St. John,

pray for us.

St. Thomas,

pray for us.

St. James,

pray for us.

St. Philip,

pray for us.

St. Bartholomew,

pray for us.

St. Matthew,

pray for us.

St. Simon,

pray for us.

St. Thaddeus,

pray for us.

St. Matthias,

pray for us.

St. Barnabas,

pray for us.

St. Luke,

pray for us.

St. Mark,

pray for us.

All holy apostles and evangelists,

pray for us.

All holy disciples of our Lord,

pray for us.

All holy innocents,

pray for us.

St. Stephen,

pray for us.

St. Lawrence,

pray for us.

St. Vincent,

pray for us.

Sts. Fabian and Sebastian,

pray for us.

Sts. John and Paul,

pray for us.

Sts. Cosmas and Damian,

pray for us.

Sts. Gervase and Protase,

pray for us.

All holy martyrs,

pray for us.

St. Sylvester,

pray for us.

St. Gregory,

pray for us.

St. Ambrose,

pray for us.

St. Augustine,

pray for us.

St. Jerome,

pray for us.

St. Martin,

pray for us.

St. Nicholas,

pray for us.

All holy bishops and confessors,

pray for us.

All holy doctors,

pray for us.

St. Anthony,

pray for us.

St. Benedict,

pray for us.

St. Dominic,

pray for us.

St. Francis,

pray for us.

All holy priests and Levites,

pray for us.

All holy monks and hermits,

pray for us.

St. Mary Magdalene,

pray for us.

St. Agatha,

pray for us.

St. Lucy,

pray for us.

St. Agnes,

pray for us.

St. Cecilia,

pray for us.

St. Catherine,

pray for us.

St. Anastasia,

pray for us.

All holy virgins and widows,
pray for us.
All holy saints of God,
make intercession for us.
Be merciful,
spare us, O Lord.
Be merciful,
graciously hear us, O Lord.
From all evil,
deliver us, O Lord.
From all sin,
deliver us, O Lord.
From your just anger,
deliver us, O Lord.
From a sudden and unprovided death,
deliver us, O Lord.
From the snares of the devil,
deliver us, O Lord.
From anger, hatred, and feelings of revenge,
deliver us, O Lord.
From everlasting death,
deliver us, O Lord.
Through the mystery of your holy incarnation,
deliver us, O Lord.
Through your coming,
deliver us, O Lord.
Through your nativity,
deliver us, O Lord.

Through your baptism and holy fasting,
deliver us, O Lord.
Through your cross and passion,
deliver us, O Lord.
Through your death and burial,
deliver us, O Lord.
Through your holy resurrection,
deliver us, O Lord.
Through your admirable ascension,
deliver us, O Lord.
Through the coming of the Holy Spirit, the comforter,
deliver us, O Lord.
In the day of judgment,
deliver us, O Lord.
We sinners,
we beseech you, hear us.
That you would spare us,
we beseech you, hear us.
That you would pardon us,
we beseech you, hear us.
That you would bring us to true penance,
we beseech you, hear us.
That you would govern and preserve your holy Church,
we beseech you, hear us.
That you would preserve our pope and all ministers,
we beseech you, hear us.
That you would give peace and true concord to Christian kings and queens,
we beseech you, hear us.

That you would grant peace and unity to all Christian people,
we beseech you, hear us.
That you would bring back to the unity of the Church all those who have strayed away and lead to the light of the gospel all unbelievers,
we beseech you, hear us.
That you would confirm and preserve us in your holy service,
we beseech you, hear us.
That you would lift up our minds to desire heaven,
we beseech you, hear us.
That you would render eternal blessing to all our benefactors,
we beseech you, hear us.
That you would give and preserve the fruits of the earth,
we beseech you, hear us.
That you would grant eternal rest to all the faithful departed,
we beseech you, hear us.
That you would graciously hear us, Son of God,
we beseech you, hear us.
Lamb of God, who takes away the sins of the world,
spare us, O Lord.
Lamb of God, who takes away the sins of the world,
have mercy on us.
Christ, hear us.
Christ, graciously hear us.
Lord, have mercy on us.
Christ, have mercy on us.
Lord, have mercy on us.
Our Father…

Let us pray:
O God, whose nature it is to have mercy and to spare, receive our petitions, that we and all your servants may, through your compassion and goodness, be mercifully absolved from all our sins and attain to eternal salvation through Christ, Our Lord. Amen.

## PRAYERS FOR THE HOLY SOULS

*Death is not the ultimate victor for the Christian. The resurrection of Jesus Christ means that* "death is swallowed up in victory" (1 Corinthians 15:54). *This is the root cause and source of our joyful hope. We pray in the risen Lord for the repose of the souls of those who have gone before us. Together one day we shall be with the Lord in heaven, where* "death shall be no more, neither shall there be mourning nor crying nor pain any more" (Revelation 21:4).

***For the Departed***

Out of the depths I cry to you, O Lord,
  Lord, hear my voice!
Let your ears be attentive
  to the voice of my supplications!
If you, O Lord, should mark iniquities,
  Lord, who could stand?
But there is forgiveness with you,
  that you may be feared.
I wait for the Lord, my soul waits,
and in his word I hope;
my soul waits for the Lord
  more than watchmen for the morning,
  more than watchmen for the morning.
O Israel, hope in the Lord!
  For with the Lord there is mercy,
  and with him is plenteous redemption.

And he will redeem Israel
from all his iniquities.

Psalm 130

O Lord, hear my prayer.
**And let my cry come to you.**

Let us pray:
O God, the Creator and Redeemer of all the faithful, grant to the souls of your servants the remission of all their sins, that through our pious supplications they may obtain that pardon they have always desired. You who live and reign for ever and ever. Amen.

***Jesu***

Jesu, by that shuddering dread which fell on thee;
Jesu, by that cold dismay which sicken'd thee;
Jesu, by that pang of heart which thrill'd in thee;
Jesu, by that mount of sins which crippled thee;
Jesu, by that sense of guilt which stifled thee;
Jesu, by that innocence which girdled thee;
Jesu, by that sanctity which reigned in thee;
Jesu, by that Godhead which was one with thee;
Jesu, spare these souls which are so dear to thee;
Who in prison, calm and patient, wait for thee;
Hasten, Lord, their hour, and bid them come to
thee.
To that glorious home, where they shall ever gaze on thee.

St. John Henry Newman

### *For Deceased Parents*

O God, who has commanded us to honor our father and mother, in your mercy have pity on the souls of my father and mother, and forgive them their sins; and bring me to see them in the joy of eternal brightness. Through Christ our Lord. Amen.

### *For Our Departed Loved Ones*

We seem to give them back to you, O God, who gave them to us. Yet as you did not lose them in giving, so do we not lose them by their return. Not as the world gives do you give, O lover of souls. What you give you do not take away, for what is yours is ours also if we are yours. And life is eternal, and love is immortal, and death is only a horizon, and a horizon is nothing save the limit of our sight. Lift us up, strong Son of God, that we may see further; cleanse our eyes that we may see more clearly; draw us closer to yourself that we may know ourselves to be nearer to our loved ones who are with you. And while you prepare a place for us, prepare us also for that happy place, that where you are we may be also for evermore. Amen.

Fr. Bede Jarrett

### *When a Baby Has Died*

Heavenly Father, your ways are hidden from our eyes. Comfort, we pray you, the parents who grieve at the loss of their baby. Grant them grace to face the future with courage and gallantry. May they understand in faith that your love, as a Father, will not cause them a needless tear and that they will meet again in a fuller life the one whose earthly body they prepared on earth.

Michael Buckley

***For All the Faithful Departed***

Receive, Lord, in tranquility and peace, the souls of your servants who have departed out of this present life to be with you. Give them the life that knows no age, the good things that do not pass away, through Jesus Christ our Lord.

St. Ignatius Loyola

***Bona Mors (Devotions for a Happy Death)***

Lord, have mercy,
Lord, have mercy.
Christ, have mercy,
Christ, have mercy.
Lord, have mercy,
Lord, have mercy.
Holy Mary,
pray for us.
All you holy angels and archangels,
pray for us.
All the choirs of the saints,
pray for us.
St. John the Baptist,
pray for us.
St. Joseph,
pray for us.
All you holy patriarchs and prophets,
pray for us.

St. Peter,

pray for us.

St. Paul,

pray for us.

St. Andrew,

pray for us.

St. John,

pray for us.

All you holy apostles and evangelists,

pray for us.

All you holy doctors of Our Lord,

pray for us.

All you holy innocents,

pray for us.

St. Stephen,

pray for us.

St. Lawrence,

pray for us.

All you holy martyrs,

pray for us.

St. Sylvester,

pray for us.

St. Gregory,

pray for us.

St. Augustine,

pray for us.

All you holy bishops and confessors,

pray for us.

St. Benedict,
pray for us.
St. Francis,
pray for us.
St. Camillus,
pray for us.
St. John of God,
pray for us.
All you holy monks and hermits,
pray for us.
St. Mary Magdalene,
pray for us.
St. Lucy,
pray for us.
All you holy virgins and widows,
pray for us.
All you saints of God,
intercede for us.
Be merciful,
spare us, O Lord.
Be merciful,
hear us, O Lord.
Be merciful,
deliver us, O Lord.
From the peril of death,
deliver us, O Lord.
From all evil,
deliver us, O Lord.

From the power of the devil,
deliver us, O Lord.
Through your nativity,
deliver us, O Lord.
Through your cross and passion,
deliver us, O Lord.
Through your death and burial,
deliver us, O Lord.
Through your glorious resurrection,
deliver us, O Lord.
Through your wonderful ascension,
deliver us, O Lord.
Through the grace of the Holy Spirit, the Comforter,
deliver us, O Lord.
Lord, have mercy on us.
Christ, have mercy on us.
Lord, have mercy on us.

We beseech your mercy, O Lord, to strengthen your servants with your grace at the hour of death, that the enemy may not prevail over us, but that we may deserve to pass with your angels into everlasting life.

Almighty and most gracious God, who brought forth for your thirsting people a stream of living water from the rock, draw tears of true repentance from our stony hearts, that we may be sorry for our sins, gain forgiveness of them from your mercy, and so attain to everlasting life.

Lord Jesus Christ, Redeemer of the world, behold us prostrate at your feet. With our whole heart we are sorry for our sins of thought, word, and deed; and because we love you and will ever love you above all created things, we are resolved, with the help of your grace, never more to offend you.

O Jesus, who during your prayer to the Father in the garden was filled with so much sorrow and anguish that your sweat became as drops of blood, have mercy on us.

Have mercy on us, O Lord; have mercy on us.

O Jesus, betrayed by the kiss of a traitor into the hands of the wicked, seized and bound like a thief, and forsaken by your disciples, have mercy on us.

Have mercy on us, O Lord; have mercy on us.

O Jesus, sentenced to death, led like a malefactor before Pilate, scorned and derided by Herod, have mercy on us.

Have mercy on us, O Lord; have mercy on us.

O Jesus, stripped of your garments and cruelly scourged at the pillar, have mercy on us.

Have mercy on us, O Lord; have mercy on us.

O Jesus, crowned with thorns, buffeted, struck with a reed, blindfolded, clothed with a purple garment, and overwhelmed with reproaches, have mercy on us.

Have mercy on us, O Lord; have mercy on us.

O Jesus, loaded with a cross and led to the place of execution as a lamb to the slaughter, have mercy on us.

Have mercy on us, O Lord; have mercy on us.

O Jesus, numbered among thieves, blasphemed and derided, offered gall and vinegar to drink, and crucified in dreadful torment from the sixth to the ninth hour, have mercy on us.

Have mercy on us, O Lord; have mercy on us.

O Jesus, who expired on the cross, was pierced with a lance in the presence of your holy mother, and from whose side poured forth blood and water, have mercy on us.

Have mercy on us, O Lord; have mercy on us.

O Jesus, taken down from the cross and bathed in the tears of your sorrowing virgin mother, have mercy on us.

Have mercy on us, O Lord; have mercy on us.

O Jesus, covered with bruises, marked with the five wounds, embalmed with spices, and laid in the sepulcher, have mercy on us.

Have mercy on us, O Lord; have mercy on us.

O Jesus, who rose from the dead by the power of the Father and so became the source of our own resurrection, have mercy on us.

Have mercy on us, O Lord; have mercy on us.

He has truly borne our sorrows.

And he has carried our griefs.

Let us pray:
O God, whose only Son, Jesus Christ, underwent death so that in his own flesh he might conquer it, help us in meditating on his passion, death, and resurrection to put aside our unholy fear of death and see it as the gateway through which we must pass in our journey to eternal life. Amen.

## ACKNOWLEDGMENTS

The compiler and publisher wish to express their gratitude to the following for permission to reproduce or adapt material of which they are the authors, publishers, or copyright holders. An asterisk indicates that the prayer has been adapted.

Excerpts from the English translation of *The Roman Missal* © 2011, International Committee on English in the Liturgy, Inc. All rights reserved.

Scripture passages have been taken from the *Revised Standard Version*, Catholic edition. Copyright 1946, 1952, 1971 by the Division of Christian Education of the National Council of Churches of Christ in the USA. Used by permission. All rights reserved.

Grateful acknowledgment is offered to:

Catholic Truth Society for one prayer from *The Simple Prayer Book*.

Fontana Paperbacks for three prayers by William Barclay from *The Plain Man's Book of Prayers*.

Lutterworth Press for three prayers by George Appleton.

Augsburg Publishing House for two prayers reprinted by permission from *Diary of Daily Prayer* by J. Barrie Shepherd, copyright Augsburg Publishing House.

McCrimmon Ltd., publishers of *The One Who Listens*, for the prayers by Michael Hollings and Etta Gullick. Used with permission. All rights reserved.

Oxford University Press for three prayers by John Baillie from *A Diary of Private Prayer* (1936) and one by Eric

Milner-White from *Daily Prayer*, edited by Eric Milner-White and G.W. Briggs (1941). Reprinted by permission of Oxford University Press.

Alfred A. Knopf, Inc. and Faber and Faber Ltd. Translation © 1964 by Alfred A. Knopf, Inc. and Faber and Faber Ltd. Reprinted from *Markings* by Dag Hammarskjold, translated by Leif Sjoberg and W. H. Auden, by permission of Alfred A. Knopf, Inc.

A. R. Mowbray & Co. Ltd. for one prayer from *Sursum Corda*.

Franciscan Herald Press for two prayers from *A Christian's Prayer Book*, compiled and edited by Peter Coughlan, Ronald C.D. Jasper, and Teresa Rodrigues, O.S.B.

St. Thomas More Centre for Pastoral Liturgy for one prayer by Harold Winstone.

Harper & Row, Publishers, Inc. for selections from *The Divine Milieu* by Pierre Teilhard de Chardin, translated by Bernard Wall, copyright 1957 by Editions du Seuil, Paris. English translation © 1960 by Wm. Collins Sons & Co., London and Harper & Row, Publishers, Inc., New York. Also for a selection from *A Gift for God* by Mother Teresa, © 1975 by Mother Teresa Missionaries of Charity. Both reprinted by permission of Harper & Row, Publishers, Inc.

Sheed and Ward Ltd. for two prayers by Caryll Houselander.

Farrar, Straus & Giroux, Inc. for selection from *Thoughts in Solitude* by Thomas Merton. © 1956, 1958 by the Abbey of Our Lady of Gethsemani. Reprinted by permission of Farrar, Straus and Giroux, Inc.

Father Peter John Cameron, O.P., *Jesus Present Before Me*, Servant Books, 2008.

Sheed and Ward for two prayers by Michel Quoist. Used by permission of Sheed and Ward, 115 E. Armour Blvd., P.O. Box 281, Kansas City, Missouri 64141-0281.

Macmillan Publishing Company for selection by Dietrich Bonhoeffer. Reprinted with permission of Macmillan Publishing Company from *Letters and Papers from Prison*, Rev., Enlarged Edition by Dietrich Bonhoeffer. © 1953, 1967, 1971 by SCM Press Ltd.

The family of Dr. L.D. Weatherhead for permission to print one prayer by Leslie Weatherhead. © Family of Dr. L.D. Weatherhead.

While every effort has been made to trace copyright holders, if there should be any error or omission, the publishers will be happy to rectify this at the first opportunity.